C0-AWF-145

Canadian Cases in Public Administration

Methuen: Canadian Politics and Government

The Provincial Political Systems: Comparative Essays
D. Bellamy, J. H. Pammett, D. C. Rowat

Politics and Government of Urban Canada: Selected Readings, 3rd Edition
L. D. Feldman, M. D. Goldrick

Public Administration in Canada: Selected Readings, 3rd Edition
W. D. K. Kernaghan

Canadian Cases in Public Administration
W. D. K. Kernaghan

The Prime Minister and the Cabinet
W. A. Matheson

Canadian Federalism: Myth or Reality, 3rd Edition
J. P. Meekison

Business and Government in Canada, 2nd Edition
K. J. Rea, J. T. McLeod

Canadian Cases in Public Administration

Kenneth Kernaghan
Brock University

Methuen
Toronto • London • Sydney • Wellington

Kernaghan, W.D.K., 1940-
Canadian cases in public administration

". . . a companion volume to the third edition of Public administration in Canada: selected readings . . ." Includes bibliographical references and index.

ISBN 0-458-92230-7

1. Public administration—Case studies. 2. Canada—Politics and government—Case studies. I. Title. II. Title: Public administration in Canada.

JL108.K475 354'.71 C77-001009-1

Printed and bound in Canada

1 2 3 4 5 81 80 79 78 77

Contents

Note

The cases in this book have been selected solely on the basis of their value for discussion and analysis. They are not intended to represent either correct or incorrect handling of administrative problems.

Subject Index

Introduction*

This book has two major purposes. One is to make available for the first time in published form a collection of Canadian case studies in public administration. The other is to stimulate government employees as well as teachers and students in universities and colleges to write additional cases.

This casebook also serves as a companion volume to the third edition of *Public Administration in Canada: Selected Readings*[1] in that the cases relate in a practical way to many of the administrative questions raised in a theoretical context in the book of readings. At the end of each chapter in the readings book, the cases most relevant to the essays in that chapter are listed.

As a guide for instructors wishing to choose a case bearing on a particular problem, a subject index of the editor's perception of the *major* concerns and problems of the cases is provided at the end of this introductory chapter. This index should assist instructors who wish the case discussions to be related as directly as possible to their lectures and assigned readings on issues and concepts in public administration.

A pressing need for case studies has arisen from the increased number of public administration courses in Canadian universities and colleges and from the accelerated growth of in-service training and development programs at all levels of Canadian government. Thus the intended audience for this book includes both potential and existing public servants. It is aimed at university and college students taking courses in public administration, public policy or public management and at government employees engaged in management education and training programs.

It is notable that despite the enormous and growing volume of case-study literature in the United States, the authors of a recent report for the National Academy of Public Administration in that country argued that:

> New case studies are needed which are based upon actual problems or issues in government and which reveal the dynamics and the constraints involved. The increased attention to complicated policy analysis has not displaced the continuing need for short, pointed examples of the human and institutional relationships, foibles, opportunities, and restrictions that case studies can provide, if properly prepared and used. There is also the need for faculty to become more adept at using case material.[2]

*This introduction is based in part on my article on "Case Research in Canadian Public Administration", *Optimum*, vol. 6, no. 2 (1975), pp. 5-20.

This book has been prepared to help achieve these ends in the field of *Canadian* public administration.

The conduct of case research in Canadian public administration is important for several reasons. First, the writing of case studies can supplement our still inadequate store of knowledge about the substance and process of public policy and management. Secondly, the use of cases can bring a real-life milieu to classroom discussions so as to join theory and practice. The case method assists students to relate abstract and theoretical concepts to concrete problems of public policy and management. Cases are valuable for students who have no practical experience in government in that they receive some vicarious experience and enhanced understanding of the challenge and intricacies of administrative issues. Cases also help to develop the students' capacity to think analytically about actual government problems. Thirdly, the case method can effectively complement the traditional lecture-seminar approach to the teaching of public administration.[3] Teachers of public administration, both in governments and in post-secondary institutions, have tended to rely to a very large extent on the more conventional teaching methods of lectures and seminars. The increased number of students in public administration who have had experience in government requires the use of a mode of teaching which allows them to make use of this experience by contributing to the discussion of problems and issues rather than listening passively to a formal lecture. Finally, government employees require increasingly sophisticated inter-personal skills to cope with changing managerial styles and new organizational forms in contemporary public services. These skills can be developed to some extent in a classroom context where individuals have the opportunity to interact with one another in the analysis of actual administrative problems and where they can benefit from an exchange of knowledge, attitudes and insights.

The cases in this volume have been gathered from disparate sources. Some cases have been written by university teachers; others by university students in public administration courses; and still others by public servants involved in government training. More than half the cases have been written by the editor of this collection. The cases have proved their value in classroom discussions where they have provided excellent opportunities for analysis of issues and concerns in public administration. All cases are based on actual events but are not exact reflections of reality in the sense of including all the facts and shades of opinion related to a particular situation. The names and departments of persons involved and the dates and places described have been disguised in most of the cases. In a few instances, however, the events and personalities are so well-known to the public that disguise would serve no useful purpose and might in fact detract from the "real-life" aura of the cases.

All the cases are set within the context of the *Canadian* political, administrative and social systems. Several of the cases provide substantial information on the structures, procedures and operations of Canadian governments. This contribution is important but it is secondary to the primary objective of providing opportunities for students of Canadian public administration to discuss and analyze accounts of actual administrative situations. In combination with lectures and assigned readings, case-study discussions can greatly enhance understanding of public administration by enabling students to relate theory to practice and the abstract to the concrete.

The remainder of this introductory section focusses on 1) the meaning of cases and the case method, 2) how to use the cases in this book, and 3) the evolution and current status of case research in Canadian public administration.

1. Cases and the Case Method

Case research involves both a type of literature (a case) and a pedagogical technique (the case method). The terms *case* and *case method* conjure up a striking variety of images in the minds of both teachers and practitioners of administration. Broadly and simply defined, a case is a description of a situation in which one or more administrators made, influenced, or implemented a decision. The case method is a group learning process in which the group members learn by analyzing a description of actual administrative situations and decisions. In their analysis and discussion of a case, group members are expected to apply ideas and insights from theoretical material presented in scholarly writings to the issues and problems contained in the case. In this way, abstract models and theories may be related to concrete situations and practical experience.

CASES

A one-sentence definition cannot depict adequately the various types of cases in use. Cases vary greatly in their form, content, length and complexity. It is clear that no single type of case is the best in all circumstances. Cases are written and selected for use according to the unique purposes of a specific course and the abilities of a particular group. Cases run the full gamut from single-page, simple management problems to book-length treatments of complicated issues of public policy and management. Most cases in administration which are designed for classroom discussion fall between these two extremes and range in length from two or three to fifty published pages.

Cases may usefully be classified according to the criteria of form and content since these criteria relate closely to the purposes which a case may serve.

In form, cases may be classified as descriptive, issue, puzzle, comprehensive or participative cases. A descriptive case provides a record of an administrative situation, including an account of the problem involved and the decision taken. The case-study group is expected to analyze critically both the decision-making process and the decision itself. An issue case describes the situation only up to the point where a decision must be made. The group is required not only to analyze the situation but also to explore the implications of possible solutions. A puzzle case is more demanding than an issue case in that the group must begin by determining what problem exists and then proceed to analyze the problem and to suggest solutions. Clearly, any of these forms of cases may involve more than one problem and may therefore require more than one decision.

The comprehensive form of case is characterized by the existence of a number of interrelated issues and problems. The group is required to single out the problems to be resolved, to analyze their interrelationships and comparative importance, and to suggest a series of decisions which, taken together, constitute a coherent solution to several related problems.

Finally, a case may be written in the form of a participative case. This form is directly related to the pedagogical technique known as role playing which is discussed later. Although many existing cases may be adapted so that members of the case-study group can act out the roles of the persons appearing in the case, the most appropriate instrument for role playing is a case written specifically for that purpose. A participative case normally includes written roles for the main people in the case. Background information on the administrative situation may also be supplied but no description of the case is provided.

Public administration cases may also be classified according to their content, not in the sense of their subject matter but in the sense of their emphasis on policy or management concerns. *Policy* cases focus primarily on policy formulation—the development, weighing and choice of policy options. The cases in the excellent American casebook, *Public Administration and Policy Development,*[4] are representative of this type. A public administration case is described as "a narrative of the events that constitute or lead to a decision by a public administrator or group of public administrators. . . . The decision problems selected for treatment involve policy rather than technical issues."[5] These cases tend to emphasize the historical, legal and institutional aspects of political and administrative decisions. The dominant emphasis is on policy considerations but many management issues are raised. There are few cases focussing on policy questions which do not have obvious or implicit consequences for management.

Policy-management cases contain a more even mix of policy and management concerns. These cases usually involve significant elements of both policy formation and policy execution. For example, the editors of *Casebook in Public Administration*[6] note that most of their cases "combine administrative history, personalities, interpersonal relations and administrative techniques. . . . The authors do not distinguish sharply between "policy" and "administration" for to do so sets up an unworkable dichotomy; rather, the attempt throughout is to emphasize the cutting edge of policy, especially in the areas of greatest controversy, for it is here that administration faces its hardest tests."[7]

Finally, *management* cases centre on one or more of the great assortment of management problems which arise in the implementation of policies and programs at varying levels of the administrative hierarchy. The significance of this type of case is explained in the book entitled *Cases in Public Management.*[8] The editors contend that "the need to focus on the first-level supervisory job and on preparation for middle management is pragmatic, and derives from the elemental fact that most participants in Public Administration programs" will either be "individuals seeking degrees prior to entry into a public job, . . . or . . . mid-careerists who interrupt their public work to upgrade their skills and perspectives."[9]

THE CASE METHOD

Like the word case, the term case method is variously interpreted. The case method is a pedagogical technique which can be distinguished from such other teaching methods as lectures, seminars, role plays, programmed instruction, simulations and so on. Several variations of the case method may also be distinguished and each requires an appropriate type of case material. By far the most prevalent version of the case method involves reading, analyzing and discussing a description of an administrative situation. Students are required to read and ponder the case on their own and then to meet with a case-study group to identify the problems, to discuss the nature and implications of these problems, to set out the points of policy and management raised by the case, to debate possible solutions, and to make a decision or decisions. This general approach may be utilized in a variety of courses for students of different levels of intellect and experience. It permits use of all the forms of cases described earlier (except the participative) and has therefore a more impressive volume of case literature to support its use.

2. How To Use the Cases in This Book

All the cases in this book fall within the categories described above as policy-management and management cases; most of the cases are of the management type and most are quite brief. The need for more lengthy and more complex policy and policy-management cases is being met by the *Case Program in Canadian Public Administration*.[10]

Case studies in public administration cannot be easily classified according to their subject matter. Most cases touch on more than one aspect of management and many cases include several management issues. For example, a single case may contain important issues of personnel, finance, organization, decision making and political-administrative relations. The focus of discussion for a case study group will depend on the purpose of the course, on the personal interests of the course instructor and of the case-study participants, and on the natural flow of discussion.

The cases in this book have been written in the form of issue or puzzle cases. Thus, the actual decision is not provided for any case and the members of the case-study group are therefore required to identify the problem or problems involved before conducting any analysis or formulating any solutions. The editor has not adopted the practice of those case-study writers who follow each case with a few questions about the case. The educational benefits of the case-study process are likely to be greater if the participants themselves are obliged to sort out the most significant problems raised by the case. The provision of questions is of course more desirable with respect to lengthy, complicated cases.

The well-known case on *The Foot and Mouth Disease Epidemic, 1952* has been included as the last case in the book. Since this case is more lengthy and more complex than the other cases and since it involves several problems, it may be preferable to discuss this case after students have gained some experience in case analysis.

The Preparation and Discussion of Cases

The two major stages of case analysis are individual preparation and group discussion. The method of analysis outlined below is intended to serve as a guide primarily for students. Instructors may wish to use some variation of this method and to provide additional directions to students.

Individual Preparation

1. Read through the case the first time to obtain a general picture of the sequence of events and of the problem(s) involved.
2. Reread the case as many times as necessary to identify the problem(s) in specific terms; to determine the responsibilities, attitudes and relationships of the actors in the case; and to become familiar with the administrative and/or political setting of the case. Make notes on these points to assist you during classroom discussion of the case.
3. Note in writing also those questions you believe should be raised

during the case discussion. For example, in regard to the first case in the book, *Dr. Stockfield's Resignation,* central questions are: "Why are the research scientists resigning? What can or should be done about this situation?" Other questions are: "Why are research scientists reluctant to use the administrative services? Why are some employees overworked while others are underemployed? Why is there such a large stock of items in the stores?"

4. Assess the relation of the events and the behaviour of individuals in the case to concepts and theories examined in lectures and assigned readings. Cases provide an opportunity to test and to understand better the utility and limitations of concepts and theories by relating abstract ideas to actual situations. For example, the case of *Dr. Stockfield's Resignation* provides an opportunity to discuss such subjects as "red tape" in government, scientists versus administrators, efficiency, economy and effectiveness, reorganization, division of labour, delegation of authority, communication, leadership style and human relations.

5. Formulate alternative courses of action to remedy the problem(s) raised in the case; evaluate the probable consequences of each alternative, including the possible obstacles to successful implementation; and then settle tentatively on the most appropriate decision(s) in the case.

Since these five steps in the individual preparation of the case serve as a basis for class discussion, it is important to make written notes—if only in point form—on your questions, observations and tentative conclusions about the case.

Group Discussion

1. Cases must be discussed in an atmosphere which is conducive to a free and frank exchange of ideas and insights. The instructor is primarily responsible for creating this mood and facilitating discussion. He must resist the temptation to intervene repeatedly in the discussion to correct what he perceives to be questionable assertions and arguments. The task of challenging and criticizing the opinions of their colleagues belongs to the students. However, an instructor may appropriately intervene for such purposes as providing clarification, encouraging shy members of the group to contribute to the discussion and restraining the "monopolists," and explaining, at the end of the discussion, important points that have been missed and relating those points to theories and concepts covered in lectures and readings. The role of the instructor is likely to be more active if the case-study participants are primarily undergraduate students rather than public employees with practical administrative experience.

2. Students in turn have a responsibility to be participants, not parasites. One of the greatest benefits of the case method of learning is that students are confronted by other students who hold different views and

different values. It is important that the participants make their values explicit, for example with respect to appropriate ethical standards for public employees, so that the value premises on which participants are basing their analysis are clear. Students who wish to improve their skills in inter-personal communication must contribute to the case discussion by explaining and defending their values and their analysis. Participation in discussion and analysis of actual administrative situations in the comparatively friendly and informal atmosphere of the classroom is good training for coping with the real world after leaving the classroom. Students who prepare well and participate actively will not only improve their communication and analytical skills but will also be stimulated to be more creative and insightful in their case analysis.

3. Students should not focus unduly on the "solution" to the case. There is not usually a single correct answer—or a simple answer—to the problem(s) posed. It is inadvisable also to restrict case discussion to criticism of the activities of the actors in the case. Students should assess what went wrong (or right) and why and then propose a solution on the basis of their knowledge of and experience in public administration.

4. Finally, students should not use "lack of information" as an excuse for difficulties in analyzing a case. Certainly students will occasionally experience frustration because a case does not provide as much information as they would like to have. Such frustration is, however, a "real-life" phenomenon. Government employees are frequently obliged to make decisions under conditions of uncertainty and with far less than complete information. It is the responsibility of the instructor to resolve disputes over conflicting assumptions made in the absence of all the facts.

3. Case Research in Canada

EVOLUTION

The story of the evolution of case research in Canadian public administration is one of sporadic, piecemeal contributions made by a few university teachers and civil servants acting in relative isolation from one another and pursuing specific, limited objectives. The situation may be explained in large part by the following factors:

- the slow development of the study of public administration in Canada;
- the institutional location of the teaching of public administration within departments of political science;
- the minimal contact between teachers of public administration and business administration;
- the limited exchanges of information and of personnel between the civil services and the universities;
- administrative secrecy in government.

The collective effect of these interrelated factors has been the absence of a sustained, systematic and co-ordinated effort to produce case-study literature on problems of public policy and management.

The study of public administration

Despite significant additions to the literature on Canadian public administration during the last decade, and especially since 1970, many important subjects still await preliminary inquiry; others urgently require study in greater depth. It is notable also that the increased publication of books and articles has not been matched by a growth in the number of case studies. This lack of progress in case research is largely a result of the longstanding neglect of the study of Canadian public administration in general and of case research in particular.

Before 1945, the number of noteworthy publications on public administration was very small. In this respect, it is fascinating to find an editorial note in the November, 1945 issue of the *Canadian Journal of Economics and Political Science* in which the editors observe that they have published a few articles on public administration and "assure members of the Civil Service, and not only senior members, that they welcome articles and short notes on administrative problems and topics. Immediately, they feel the need for many studies of wartime administration before those who took part in it have forgotten what happened."[11] This editorial invitation brought forth little response from public administrators. There was a small pool of civil servants from whom contributions could be solicited and there was a reluctance among Canadian civil servants, which still exists, to commit to paper their knowledge of government. This state of affairs is especially unfortunate because "the essential contribution case studies can make to science rests in the discovery and presentation of detailed knowledge of the working of the governmental process—knowledge that might otherwise be lost or kept in the private possession of agencies, officials or other direct participants."[12]

In the 1960's, the rapid expansion of existing universities and the creation of many new universities were accompanied by an unprecedented influx of academic scholars. This development augured well for increased research in all academic fields, including public administration. However, the growth in the staff of departments of political science, which monopolized the teaching of public administration, coincided with a shift in the research and teaching interests of many political scientists. The traditional focus on government institutions, structures and constitutions was displaced by an emphasis on voting studies, the legislative process and public attitudes which reflected the current research interests of American political scientists. Such Canadian issues as French-English relations of federal-provincial liaison also consumed much of the research and publication efforts of political scientists during this period. The decade of the 1960's did not therefore provide fertile ground for cultivating research in public administration. However, some of the seeds planted during this period did bear fruit in the 1970s.

During the post-war period, the prime mover in keeping the study of public administration alive has been the Institute of Public Administration of Canada. Through its annual conferences, regional groups, and research and publication programs, the Institute has brought academics and practitioners together for a productive exchange of opinion and information. Moreover, the Institute has been the source of the bulk of the literature on public administration through the publication of the proceedings of its annual conferences from 1949 to 1957 and its quarterly journal *Canadian Public Administration* beginning in 1958. The first volumes of the Canadian Public Administration Series, which had its origins in the 1960s, were published after 1970.

Given the scarcity of published materials on Canadian public administration, university teachers as well as civil servants responsible for in-service training and development have relied heavily on American and, to a lesser extent, British literature. While this dependent relationship has lessened somewhat in recent years, Canadians have until very recently depended on American case studies in public administration. Until the establishment in 1975 of the Case Program in Canadian Public Administration, there was no case-research program in Canada equivalent to the Inter-University Case Program (ICP) founded in the United States in 1951.

The first mention in a Canadian publication of case research in public administration appears to be the passing reference in J. E. Hodgetts' 1957 article on "The Civil Service and Policy Formation."[14] He notes that "case studies of actual administrative choices leading up to policy decisions are appearing in even larger numbers, and are often used as supplements to regular textbook fare."[15] His footnote reference here, however, is to the American cases contained in the Stein casebook and produced by the ICP. More by accident than design, a few books and articles were published in Canada during the 1950's and 1960's which could be used as case studies. For example, about half a dozen of the 52 selections in the 1960 book of readings on Canadian public administration edited by J. E. Hodgetts and D. C. Corbett[16] could be viewed as case studies. There is little evidence, however, that these selections were widely used for that purpose.

In the rare situations where university teachers were involved in the education of civil servants, there was greater acceptance of the case method. In the early 1960's, the management training community in the federal government began to make increasing use of case studies and even to write some brief management cases. Also, a few university teachers collected Canadian cases for classroom use. Easily the most notable efforts in this area were made by Professors D. C. Rowat and A. M. Willms of Carleton University who supplemented cases written in the public service by editing case studies written by their students.

Public administration and political science

The collection of public administration cases and the use of the case method by political scientists were clearly isolated practices. As we have already observed, the institutional locus of public administration has been within political science departments. Indeed, Carleton University's School of Public Administration, the first formal school in the country, remained an integral part of the Department of Political Science from its creation in 1953 until its separation from the Department in 1972.

It is understandable that teachers of public administration, most of whom are still trained in political science, should emphasize the political, policy and institutional aspects of public bureaucracy rather than the organizational, procedural and technical concerns of public management. The focus has been on policy formation rather than policy implementation.

Furthermore, teachers of public administration have been disposed to emulate the teaching methods of their political science colleagues by relying on formal lectures or on seminar discussions based on books and articles. There has been little incentive to depart from these pedagogical techniques to utilize cases and the case method. Political scientists teaching public administration seemed to be unaware of the case method or unwilling to use it. In any event, there has been insufficient case-study literature on Canadian problems to support active use of the case method.

Public administration and business administration

The isolation of public administration from developments in the substance and pedagogy of business administration also militated against the use of the case method in public administration. The perception that public administration was in both its intellectual and institutional dimensions a sub-field of the discipline of political science impeded contacts between teachers of business and public administration.

Moreover, while public administration was searching for its identity *vis-à-vis* political science and administration during the 1960's, business administration in Canada was preoccupied with its own problems of identity and program content. The relationship of business administration to public administration was not a major concern of business schools during this period.

During the immediate post-war years, teachers of business administration in Canada relied on case studies written primarily in the United

States (and especially at Harvard). Unlike the situation in public administration, some business schools in Canada initiated programs to produce Canadian case materials. The most successful of these programs was developed by the School of Business at the University of Western Ontario which is now the dominant institution in case research in Canadian business administration.

University teachers and administrative practitioners

For a variety of reasons there has been little exchange of information, ideas and insights between teachers and practitioners of public administration in Canada. This situation has been to the great detriment of the mutually beneficial intermixture of theory and practice in public administration. The fault for this situation must be shared by both sides. With some exceptions, the academic specialist and the administrative practitioner have neither sought nor taken up opportunities to learn from one another. Admittedly, the opportunities have been limited. Before the mid-1960's, few university teachers were involved in mid-career training programs for public servants where the classroom offered an opportunity for the confrontation and synthesis of academic perspectives and practical experience. Moreover, few teachers of public administration have had experience in government service either on an internship basis while seeking their Ph.D. degree or on an interchange basis during their teaching career. As a result, some university teachers have inadequate knowledge and understanding of the real world of public bureaucracy.

In some instances, this lack of information and of opportunities to acquire it has affected adversely the accuracy and relevance of the content of courses and has led to undue dependence on highly descriptive or highly theoretical treatments of the subject matter of public administration. Since much teaching and research in public administration has been done by teachers with little or no experience in government service, it is not surprising that the case method, which relies on narratives of actual administrative situations, has not taken root in the university community.

It is, however, precisely through the writing of cases and the use of the case method that teachers and students can experience vicariously the complexities, difficulties and opportunities of decision making in government. To produce cases of the variety required, teachers must secure the assistance of those public officials who have been personally involved in noteworthy administrative situations or who can provide case writers with access to the necessary information.

Secrecy in government

The tradition and practice of administrative secrecy in Canada has plagued social scientists generally and has been especially bothersome to researchers in public administration. Indeed, one reason why the study of public administration has suffered compared to other areas of the social sciences is that the data needed for research are more difficult to obtain.

The writing of good case studies depends to a large extent on gaining adequate access to government documents and files. Since little effort has been made to conduct case research and thereby to test the extent of the access problem, we cannot conclude that administrative secrecy has been a major obstacle to the writing of case studies. However, access to documents and clearance of cases for distribution are very important potential problems to which case writers must be sensitive. Some cases written for training purposes within the government have not been released for use because of possible embarrassment to officials involved in the cases. Recent experience suggests that most of the difficulties of confidentiality and access may be overcome by cooperation and consultation between case writers and public officials.

The Current Situation

During the past few years, there has been substantial change in the conditions which have impeded the development of case research in Canadian public administration. A number of developments have culminated in the creation and growth of the Case Program in Canadian Public Administration which may serve as a foundation for greatly expanded use of the case method and of Canadian cases in public policy and public management both within the universities and government.

First, there has been a small but significant increase in the number of scholars and students interested in public administration and a consequent expansion of literature and university courses in this field. While there has not been a proprotionate growth in the quantity of case studies, the environment in government and in the universities is now much more conducive to the writing and use of cases. The continuing neglect of case research in most universities when inquiry into public administration generally is increasing may be explained in part by the lack of a tradition of case writing. Even more important, however, was the absence of a publication and distribution outlet for cases in public administration, with the exception of full-length books or articles where the narrative of the case is normally set within a conceptual framework. There was little incentive to redirect one's research efforts toward the production of a form of literature for which there was a market but no vehicle for distribution. That vehicle now exists in the form of the Case Program in Canadian Public Administration.

Secondly, since the mid-1960's there has been a reassessment of the nship between political science and public administration. The alteration in institutional arrangements is more noticeable than that in academic relationships. A variety of new institutional designs has weakened the organizational links between public administration and departments of political science. It has increasingly been argued that administration is a generic concept in that all forms of administration, whether business, public, educational or other forms, have more similarities than differences. This belief has led to the establishment of faculties and schools of administrative studies or management in which all students take a common core of courses and are then permitted to specialize in one or more forms or areas of administration, including public administration. Another related consequence has been the creation of schools of public administration which retain courses in political science as an important component of their program but require courses from other disciplines (e.g. economics, statistics, social psychology). The program is interdisciplinary and its organization is often on an interdepartmental basis. The program emphasis may lean toward either a professional or an academic bias.

For some of the reasons outlined above, as well as the fact that the conduct of case research is expensive and time-consuming, these newly established schools have not developed extensive case programs. However, their more professional perspective and their closer contacts with business administration and with administrative practitioners have stimulated more interest in the writing and classroom use of case studies.

Thirdly, the creation of new institutions for the study of public administration and the reorganization of existing programs have established stronger structural and intellectual ties between public administration and business administration. These bonds have become especially close in situations where public administration has been grouped with business administration and possibly other forms of administration under the same roof, for example, in a Faculty of Administrative Studies. Students interested in any form of administration take a number of "core" courses deemed to constitute the heart of administration viewed as a generic concept. Even when a school of public administration has been established as an entity distinct from both political science and business administration, there is usually agreement on a common core of required subjects, several of which coincide with the core courses in schools or faculties of administration.

Overlap in the substantive content of public and business administration programs has resulted also from the expansion in both programs of courses in government-business relations. The accelerated pace of interaction between government and business officials will forge tighter links between public and business administration regardless of the organizational arrangements for the teaching of public administration.

These developments have significant implications for case research. The blurring of the interface between the public and private sectors of society requires that students, whether in schools of public or business administration, understand both (1) the political and administrative institutions and processes of government and (2) the structures and operations of large and small business organizations. A potentially effective means of achieving these objectives is to utilize case studies which explore the nature of the relations between government and business.

Although closer ties between public and business administration will weaken the organizational bonds between political science departments and public administration, they may at the same time, paradoxically, strengthen the intellectual status of public administration within the discipline of political science. It has been primarily the management component and the practical bent of public administration which has made teachers of this subject uneasy residents in the house of political science. If the management element can be hived off to schools of public administration, political scientists can focus on what they generally view as their proper concern, namely the political and policy role of the bureaucracy. Canadian political scientists may benefit also from an evaluation of the pedagogic and scientific purposes of utilizing case studies on public policy formation in political science courses.[17]

Fourthly, intellectual and personal ties are gradually being developed between university teachers and administrative practitioners. The opportunities for such contacts offered by the seminar and research activities of the Institute of Public Administration are still a very important influence. The single greatest span in the bridge between academic specialists and public servants, however, may well be in the increasing opportunities for university teachers to spend some time in government service. Many teachers have served governments in an advisory or consultative capacity but there is no more effective means of bridging theory and practice than obliging theoreticians to take up administrative posts in the public service—and obliging practitioners to put up with them. Another promising development is the introduction of internships of varying lengths of time for students enrolled in graduate programs in public administration.

All these developments will foster a larger measure of reality and relevance in the academic/professional pursuit of education in public administration. They will also stimulate and facilitate the writing and the use of case studies in university and government courses.

Finally, public officials seem to be increasingly receptive to the requests of researchers for access to government documents. Most scholars and public administrators recognize the need to preserve the confidentiality of certain classes of government information while agreeing that access to documents is on the whole unnecessarily restricted.

The expansion of case research in Canadian public administration will require careful selection of the cases to be written and agreement on the procedures for clearance and distribution. Although it is desirable to maintain the reality of a case in as many respects as possible, the release of some cases may require that the names of departments, persons, places and dates be altered. Cases can usually be disguised in this fashion without reducing significantly the value of the cases. It seems reasonable to suggest that senior administrators should be especially supportive of the writing and publication of case studies because the case method is such a potentially effective technique for training future administrators.

NOTES

[1]W. D. K. Kernaghan (ed.), *Public Administration in Canada: Selected Readings,* 3rd edition, Toronto, Methuen, 1977.

[2]Richard L. Chapman and Frederic N. Cleaveland, *Meeting the Needs of Tomorrow's Public Service: Guidelines for Professional Education in Public Administration,* National Academy of Public Administration, Washington, 1973, p. 34.

[3]For elaboration on these pedagogical purposes of using case studies and for an explanation of the scientific and operational purposes of cases, see Edwin A. Bock, "Case Studies about Government: Achieving Realism and Significance" in Edwin A. Bock, ed., *Essays on the Case Method,* Syracuse, The Inter-University Case Program, 1962, pp. 89-119.

[4]Harold Stein, ed., *Public Administration and Policy Development,* Harcourt, Brace, Inc., New York, 1952.

[5]*Ibid.,* p. xxvii. The length of the cases ranges from 10 to 88 pages and the average length is about 30 pages. The few British and Australian casebooks available are similar in emphasis and length. For Britain, *see* F. M. G. Willson and Gerald Rhodes, *Administrators in Action,* volume 1, George Allen and Unwin, London, 1961. *Administrators in Action,* volume 2, George Allen and Unwin, London, 1965. For Australia, *see* B. B. Shaffer and D. C. Corbett, *Decisions: Case Studies in Australian Public Administration,* F. W. Cheshire, Melbourne, 1965.

[6]R. Joseph Novogrod, Marshall Edward Dimock and Gladys Ogden Dimock, *Casebook in Public Administration,* Holt, Rinehart and Winston, New York, 1969.

[7]*Ibid.,* pp. v and vi. The length of the cases range from 8 to 32 pages and the average length is about 18 pages.

[8]Robert T. Golembiewski and Michael White, eds., *Cases in Public Management,* Rand McNally & Co., Chicago, 1973.

[9]*Ibid.,* p. xxi. The length of these cases ranges from 2 to 27 pages and the average length is about 5 pages.

[10]This Program is sponsored jointly by the Public Service Commission of Canada and the Institute of Public Administration of Canada. Existing cases and information on this Program may be obtained by contacting the Director, Case Program in Canadian Public Administration, 897 Bay St., Toronto, Ontario.

[11]Vol. 11, no. 4, November, 1945, p. 523.

[12]Edwin A. Bock, "Case Studies and Government," p. 105.

[13]"Dives and Lazarus: Three Reports on the Teaching of Political Science," *Canadian Journal of Economics and Political Science,* vol. 23, no. 1, February, 1952, p. 92.

[14]J. E. Hodgetts, "The Civil Service and Policy Formation," *Canadian Journal of Economics and Political Science,* vol. 23, no. 4, November, 1957, pp. 467-479.

[15]*Ibid.,* p. 468.

[16]*Canadian Public Administration,* The Macmillan Company of Canada, Toronto, 1960.

[17]For an excellent analysis of this question, *see* Edwin A. Bock, "Improving the Usefulness of the Case Study in Political Science," in D. M. Freeman, ed., *Introduction to the Science of Politics,* The Free Press, New York, 1974. *See* also such case-study books in political science as James B. Christoph and Bernard E. Brown, eds., *Cases in Comparative Politics,* Little Brown and Company, Boston, 2nd ed., 1969; Harold Stein, ed., *American Civil-Military Decisions: A Book of Case Studies,* University of Alabama Press, Alabama, 1963; and Edwin A. Bock and Alan K. Campbell, eds., *Case Studies in American Government,* Prentice-Hall, Englewood Cliffs, N.J., 1962.

1

Dr. Stockfield's Resignation

Dr. James Burroughs is the director of a large government research laboratory located some thirty miles from Canfield, a city in Eastern Canada with a population of just over 200,000. The laboratory is divided into six functional branches whose job is mainly applied research in the radio and electronics fields. The total staff of the laboratory is about five hundred.

One morning about two weeks ago, Dr. Eric Stockfield, one of the top research scientists and assistant head of the Space Research Branch, came to Burrough's office to announce that he would be leaving the laboratory in a month's time. In his interview with Burroughs, Stockfield stated that he was leaving to take a job with a United States firm at a higher salary. He gave the following, however, as the main reason for his departure:

> While the research problems here are interesting and challenging, and I like working here, I cannot achieve the results that I feel I should achieve; both I and my branch are constantly burdened with what are essentially clerical and handicraft jobs. Furthermore, we have difficulty getting the right kind of equipment and supplies. As you know, our last order for equipment had to be sent back because it did not meet our specifications, and even in smaller items we don't get what we want. Requisitions for supplies and services are sometimes changed without consultation. Instead of spending our time looking at research, the chief and I spend more time on petty details of administration. I get very tired of fighting red tape.

Dr. Burroughs was concerned about the loss of Stockfield and about his complaints. He had heard complaints before but he considered these to be the normal difficulties of administration in a bureaucracy and he had not paid them too much heed. Usually he had referred gripes to the head of Administrative Services and they seemed to be settled there. Three years before, after discussing the problem of administrative services with some of his senior people, he had persuaded Treasury Board and the Public Service Commission to give them a senior position for a head of an Administrative Services Branch. They had recruited a bright young administrator named Ted Paxton who had gained recognition in another government department. Paxton had then taken over what had been a rather loosely scattered group of services; he had worked very hard organizing the Branch and had appeared to fit into the organization well. At first there had been some laudatory comments from senior scientists but these had not been repeated after the first six months.

Burroughs himself had noticed that the other branches sometimes seemed reluctant to use the administrative services. He had, for instance, noticed on one of his visits to a lab that a scientist was busy with a soldering iron wiring a piece of equipment. "Why do *you* have to do that?" he had asked. The reply was: "For two reasons: first, Technical Services are too busy and we can't wait, and second, their technicians don't know too much about transistors."

The day after Stockfield's visit, Dr. Burroughs called on Ted Paxton to discuss the administrative services. Paxton was quite convinced that his branch was doing a good job. He stressed the fact that he had been able to reduce the services staff by almost ten per cent in three years and had achieved other economies. "After all," he said, "the job of this Branch is to provide administrative services to the labs at minimum cost." He then produced a letter from headquarters, which Burroughs had already seen, complimenting the laboratory on having had the lowest ratio of overhead costs to laboratory staff in the previous year. Dr. Burroughs agreed that the objective of the laboratory was to achieve appropriate research results at minimum cost, and that the object of Paxton's branch was to provide the services to achieve this general objective, but he wondered whether the services were adequate. Burroughs asked whether Paxton still countersigned all requisitions himself. Paxton assured him that he did and that he sometimes handled as many as fifty requisitions in a day. Moreover he looked after all complaints. Burroughs accepted Paxton's offer to take him on a tour of the branch and discuss its work in more detail.

They visited the Technical Services first and found several technicians extremely busy, even harassed. The supervisor explained: "These men are electronic technicians and most of the current projects seem to require electronic equipment. We have been extremely busy for over a year now. The lads often work overtime but I still have to shift priorities continually to try and keep the scientists happy." He admitted that other sections were not so busy and that two men who were glass blowers had been on make-work for some time.

The director and Paxton visited the Personnel Office and Central Registry next. The Personnel Office was staffed by one personnel officer and five clerks. Each clerk was assigned a specific job: one was responsible for pay, another leave and attendance, a third recruitment, a fourth superannuation and a fifth promotions and reclassifications. They were all in one room for they had to use the same card and personnel files. Paxton explained that he had removed the partitions of individual offices when he first came because it was ridiculous for each man to trot in and out of his office to get the records he required. Thus a considerable saving in space had been achieved.

Central Registry had a staff of more than thirty and appeared to be quite efficient. Specific times were fixed for mail in and out, for messenger rounds and for receiving requests for file loans. Mail was registered in and correspondence requiring a reply was noted. Outgoing mail was scrutinized and the incoming register checked to make sure that all mail had been answered. If a letter remained unanswered for more than a week, the guilty officer was reminded every three days until he replied to the letter or sent a memo explaining the circumstances. The public relations of the lab had been considerably enhanced by this measure. Paxton stated that he had all the incoming mail delivered to the scientists on the day it arrived. This same-day delivery had not always been achieved previously. There were also six messenger runs to all labs every day instead of the casual 'on-request' service formerly provided. Paxton had asked the head of Central Registry to study different classification systems and to redesign the present filing codes as soon as possible. He had reorganized Central Registry into functional groups, each specializing in one records job. At the end of the discussion Paxton mentioned that:

> The clerks in the Personnel Office and the Central Registry are bored with their jobs; they seize upon every opportunity to gossip with people visiting the office. Unfortunately, while there are peak load periods in most of the sections when the clerks are asked to work hard, there are often rather slack periods as well. The supervisors can't always look after the slack units for they have to pitch in and help the busy sections.

Burroughs and Paxton next visited the Property Management Unit which consists of Building Maintenance and Site Maintenance. The Building Maintenance section included a staff of painters, carpenters, electricians, plumbers, etc. They worked to a production control system with work measurement standards for every job. Burroughs was aware that his labs were known for their neat appearance and good upkeep. In fact, a visiting scientist had once told him: "The painters seem to do a repainting job here almost before the last one has properly dried." The Site Maintenance Section had a fleet of bulldozers, scrapers, snowmobiles and other vehicles. A staff of mechanics was busy working on them and the equipment looked in beautiful condition. The foreman explained that his staff was not very busy during the summer but that they were extremely busy during the winter when a lot of snow clearing had to be done.

The Transport Section and the Purchasing and Supply Section were housed in one building so they were visited together. Burroughs found nothing of note in the Transport unit. In the Purchasing and Supply Section, however, he was startled to find that the stores carried over 200,000 items and that the primary task of keeping the stores up-to-date by posting entries on stock record cards required the service of seven clerks. It seemed to Burroughs that a large proportion of the stock had not been moved recently and Paxton admitted that the requirements of the labs change rather quickly, but that he had not yet found a system for getting rid of out-of-date items. He said that he would see to this immediately. Burroughs noted that the Purchasing Officers were busy compiling lists of items required by the labs and procuring and entering the list prices of the products of various manufacturers. Paxton pointed out what a great range of prices many of the items had, and added: "We can save a great deal of money by getting a comparable item for our officers. Of course we get complaints that the items are not what was ordered, but I don't think the scientists can really tell the difference if they don't look at the labels."

The final visit was to Office Services Section. At Paxton's suggestion the stenos and typists have been collected in a central pool; only senior men retained their secretaries. In the pool, Patrick Dunn, the supervisor, told them that he had a production control system and that the average production per girl was one of the highest in the government. Dunn explained that he kept the girls working full time by having the officers note the priority of the typing. High priorities were done immediately but the regular priority material was allowed to accumulate so that there would always be a backlog of work. Burroughs inquired whether there were any complaints and Dunn replied: "Sure there are complaints, but this is the way scientists are; they want everything yesterday. We know from experience what items are not urgent and we act accordingly. Besides many of the scientists complain because they want to have their secretaries back—to brew their coffee for them." Burroughs asked Paxton whether other clerical services such as duplicating, drafting and so on were provided, but Paxton explained that many of the branches had their own duplicators and that there seemed to be no need for other clerical services. He added that the duplicators now in use were getting pretty old and that he had no plans to replace them. When they were worn out he would centralize duplicating services, with a large new Xerox installation that would be much better than the outdated copiers now in use. He had his eye on a bright young man in Registry who would make a good job of this service.

When Dr. Burroughs returned to his office, he found another scientist from Stockfield's branch waiting to see him. This man was a promising researcher who had left a university post to come to the lab. With some hesitation he explained that he had applied for another teaching post and had been accepted. He said that when he left the university he had no real conception of what working for the government would be like. When Burroughs questioned him, he blurted out: "I think the real trouble here is the administration; if only each branch were allowed to run its own show completely, the boys would be a lot happier." He had nothing against Paxton whom he considered "a fine young man", but he felt that the administrative systems were being "strangled by red tape."

2

The Shared Authority

The setting for this case is a high-ranking historical museum, which attracts visitors from across Canada and throughout the world. It is in a large city whose council has always voted the funds necessary for its operation but has never paid any attention to the details of its management. The building was the bequest many years ago of a wealthy citizen.

The management of the museum is the responsibility of a Civic History Committee which, for all practical purposes, is self-perpetuating although city council has a theoretical veto of appointments to the committee. The committee solicits funds from large businesses which profit from tourism, obtains the remainder of the required funds from city hall, and hears reports from its secretary who is responsible for the administration of the museum. The committee usually meets once a year, and its chairman acts as chief canvasser for funds and convener of meetings.

The secretary, Dr. Flagge, is a recognized scholar with several publications to his credit who takes a keen interest in the performance and reputation of the museum. He devotes only part of his time to museum management, about the equivalent of one day a week, and receives a small honorarium. His earnings from royalties and research for an encyclopedia firm are his main income. He works in a room with a private entrance at the back of the museum, and he seldom appears in the museum during the day. In the evenings the janitors frequently see him wandering around, inspecting the exhibits with loving care. He is always available to see the three senior members of the museum staff and often makes sound suggestions. He banks the receipts for Mrs. Mooney and helps her with accounts when necessary. The junior members of the staff hardly know that he exists.

Reporting directly to Dr. Flagge are Mr. Leduc, Mr. Martin and Mrs. Mooney. All three have been at the museum for over five years—Martin has been there for eighteen years—and all three have good reputations. In fact the chairman of the Civic History Committee told city council at the last budget meeting that they were fortunate in having a staff whose avowed goal was to make the museum the oustanding institution of its kind.

Mrs. Mooney manages a canteen and souvenir shop for visitors, which has a turnover of up to one thousand dollars on holidays during the summer; Mr. Martin handles the displays and building maintenance; and Mr. Leduc is in charge of the guides and of public relations. Mrs. Mooney has had a staff of girls, varying from six in the summer months to two in winter. Mr. Martin usually has had four or five men to assist him. Mr. Leduc has had as many as seven guides in the rush time and two or three in the off season, in addition to one full-time man for publicity and a commissionaire at the front door. Martin's display men are often called on to assist Leduc in preparing signs or other publicity material.

This year the city council failed, for the first time, to give the committee the money it asked for. The council voted to give the museum the same amount as last year and thereby left the budget short by over ten thousand dollars. In order to maintain the standards of the museum, Dr. Flagge decided to reorganize. He planned to cut the canteen staff to two, Mrs. Mooney and one assistant, with the idea that a system of rotation could be worked out so that there would always be one or two of the female guides to help out in the canteen when necessary. Likewise he decided to cut Martin's staff to three, retaining Martin and the two best display men, with the understanding that Martin should use the male guides to help him when they were not too busy. Mr. Leduc was to have ten guides in the summer and six or seven in the winter time. About half the number of guides would be female.

Having cleared these ideas with the chairman of the committee, Dr. Flagge called a conference of his three supervisors. This was a unique event. He explained his ideas in detail and stated that by following his plan at least ten thousand dollars a year in wages could be saved. Tourists, he pointed out, tend to arrive in crowds on the weekends while museum traffic slows down during the week. Therefore Martin could get the displays prepared and major building maintenance done during the slack period while the women handled the tours. On the weekend the men could shoulder most of the guiding duties while some of the women guides moved into the canteen to help with the rush there. Dr. Flagge also asked Leduc and Mrs. Mooney to keep overtime to a minimum and encourage staff to take their days off during the week in lieu of overtime. He praised the staff for their work and said that the committee was agreed that the next budget, now in preparation, would have a salary increase for the three supervisors though the amounts could not be fixed until after the city council had passed the budget. They all agreed to the new plan, and Mr. Leduc was given the responsibility for arranging the flexible timetable that would be necessary.

Despite the good intentions the new plan did not work out. The women were happy. They seemed to enjoy the guiding as a change from canteen work and had no trouble accepting the supervision of either Leduc or Mrs. Mooney. But Mr. Martin found it difficult to adjust. He seemed unable to arrange his workload so that the burden fell during the week, and there was constant bickering with Mr. Leduc about the amount of time the men spent under his direction. Martin felt that they did not do a fair share of the maintenance, and whenever he had planned a major work on displays he was frustrated by men taking their days off. He found it necessary to conscript a guide for urgent chores without consulting Leduc, who also took his days off during the week. Leduc found this very inconvenient, and once or twice visitors had left because there were no guides available. A few times Mrs. Mooney saw the trouble and sent one of her girls over to help with the guiding. There were a number of discussions among the three supervisors but the difficulty persisted.

The situation was complicated by personal factors. Both Leduc and Martin are in the militia. Leduc, a university graduate, now only 32 years old, holds the rank of major while Martin, a man of 45, has never been able to pass his captaincy exams. Martin showed his sensitivity when dealing with guides, who were often history graduates, by referring to the ineffectiveness of their book-learning when practical problems came up.

In early summer Mr. Leduc was away for five days to attend a conference of the learned societies. He had volunteered to go, offering to pay his own hotel expenses if the committee would defray travelling costs. This arrangement had been made every year since Leduc had come to the museum and, as always, he left his senior guide, a Mr. Burch, in charge of the guides. As soon as Leduc left difficulties arose. Mr. Martin and Mr. Burch could not agree on work schedules, and one afternoon an ugly scene took place in the museum. Unfortunately the incident was reported to the local press, which made a feature story out of the dissension in the museum. Martin was quoted as criticizing the guiding arrangements and staff. Furthermore, the wife of a committee member had heard some of the dispute; her husband called on the chairman that evening and together they went to see the secretary. On the way over they had pretty well made up their minds that Mr. Burch would have to be fired, for their impression was that he had acted as "an impertinent and cocky young devil". Furthermore, while they knew Martin to be a bit cranky, they also knew that he was one of the best display men in the business and would be very difficult to replace. Above all, they tried to impress on the secretary that something tangible must be done to reassure city hall. The secretary wasn't so sure that firing Burch was the answer; he thought that this was merely a minor incident but suggested he talk to the staff and report back to the chairman within two days.

Leduc was back on the job the next morning and Flagge called him to the office. They discussed the incident and Flagge soon became aware that there were more serious problems than he had known. Furthermore, Leduc said that if Burch were fired he too would go, for Burch had been acting in his name, and the criticisms of guiding arrangements in the press were also criticisms of himself. He felt that Martin must take the blame. To the secretary's question about leaving Burch in charge he replied that someone had to coordinate the guiding in his absence, and Martin was not prepared to do this; moreover Martin never came to the museum on weekends when most of the supervision was required.

As soon as Leduc left Dr. Flagge's office, Martin appeared. He explained the incident at some length and blamed Burch for his insolence: "He acted as though he were my superior." As he became more excited Martin almost broke into tears. He pointed out that he was being treated unfairly, that Leduc was getting all the trips away, and that the staff was taking it for granted that Leduc was being groomed to succeed the secretary. He went on to point out that, despite the fact that his work had been praised repeatedly, he had had no salary increase for five years, that salaries were lower than elsewhere and that the museum had no pension arrangements. He had stuck with it through thick and thin for almost twenty years. The secretary took the outburst calmly and refused to be drawn into any discussion of the incident. When Martin left, he sat back to think about the problem.

3

Dr. Aphid's Accident

Dr. B. W. Aphid is a research officer in the Regional Field Division of the Department of National Resources. The main function of this unit is to compile data for the Mapping Division, and for this purpose teams are formed which go out into the field for six months in the summer. Dr. Aphid, though only 30 years old, has been a team leader for two years; he is industrious, capable and well liked. He also has a reputation for strong views on almost any subject that comes up. One illustration of this is his reaction to car seat belts. These were put on all National Resources vehicles, and an instruction was issued that they must be used at all times when driving in a government vehicle. Dr. Aphid claims he witnessed a fatal motor accident in which the driver was pinned by the steering column because he was wearing a seat belt, and he now refuses to use a seat belt despite the departmental ruling. The division head knows this but feels there is no point in making an issue of it.

This past summer Dr. Aphid was on a series of surveys with two student assistants in an area relatively close to headquarters; the furthest he would be away was 700 miles. As usual he planned well for the tour. Among other things he had one of the lads test their main vehicle, a station wagon, and was told that it was fine except that the brakes seemed weak; the pedal had to be pressed to the floor before they would take hold and then they seemed to grab. So Dr. Aphid sent a work order to the Administrative Officer asking for the brakes to be repaired. The AO noted the request and instructed one of the prevailing rate employees to take the wagon to a garage. For some reason the work was not done.

Since one of the students was driving, Aphid did not realize that the brakes were still faulty until they had been on the survey for two or three days. When he discovered the state of affairs he remarked on it to his men and included some harsh comments in his memo to headquarters that weekend, but as there was no good opportunity to get the car repaired, he decided to let it go until rainy weather would allow time to go into a town.

Two weeks later the group found itself within 150 miles of home, and on Friday afternoon Dr. Aphid decided to go home. He had several things to do at headquarters, and he was determined to exchange the vehicle for one that was safer. The two men volunteered to stay and finish a section of the survey that afternoon and arranged to meet Aphid in the nearest town on Sunday evening.

Friday afternoon was very hot and on the way home Aphid decided to stop in one of the towns to pick up a case of beer before the stores closed for the day. To do this he had to go to a village about five miles from his quickest route, but he felt it would be well worthwhile. But in the village his luck ran out. As he was leaving the parking lot of the Brewers Retail store, his brakes failed to hold, and he was hit by a car that was driving down Main Street at about 30 miles an hour. The impact catapulted him through the windshield so that he incurred extensive facial lacerations and smashed his knee. The impact also smashed the case of beer, which Aphid had carefully put behind the driver's seat. The vehicle reeked of beer, and the inside was strewn with full and broken bottles. This fact was given particular prominence in a local press description of the accident.

The following week a member of the Opposition asked a question in the House of Commons about the use of government vehicles to transport liquor. In the question the member managed to bring out the most damaging elements of the case: namely, that the driver had not used his seat belt as required, that he was miles from his place of duty at 5.30 p.m. on a working day, and that it seemed that he had been drinking. The minister sent the question to the deputy minister with a request for an explanation. This request soon reached the Director of the Regional Field Division, who knew most of the facts. He reported these to the Deputy, together with the forecast that Dr. Aphid would be in hospital for over two months and that the damage to his knee was such that it was unlikely he would ever be able to do survey work again. The two automobiles were seriously damaged, and the other driver's lawyer had intimated that his client would be suing the department for medical damages and loss of income.

When the Deputy received the Director's report, he asked the Chief of Personnel to investigate the need for disciplinary action against any of the people involved. In the meantime Dr. Aphid had his lawyer send a claim to the department for his painful injuries and his projected loss of income, which the lawyer estimated would amount to more than $100,000.

4

The Frustrated Purchasing Agent

Mr. Jones was the Purchasing Agent for a small federal Crown Company (700 employees). In this capacity, he was responsible for all purchasing required by the Company, including such things as office supplies, office machinery and plant equipment.

The routine as laid down in a departmental manual required Mr. Jones, on receipt of a purchase requisition from one of the branches of the Company, to consult the sources of supply by calling for prices either by invitation or by public competitive tenders. The choice of procedure depended on the quantity and total dollar value of the item. For large expenditures, public tenders would be called and for smaller expenditures, tenders would be invited from at least three sources of supply. When the Purchasing Agent had studied all the tenders, he would recommend the most economical bid while taking into consideration the delivery date. The order would be typed out in the name of the recommended bidder, the bids would be attached to the Company purchase order form, and all papers would be referred to the Treasurer of the Company for purchase approval. If the purchase was approved by the Treasurer (often it was not), he would certify that enough funds were available for the purchase, and all papers would be returned to the Purchasing Agent, Mr. Jones, in order that he might proceed to place the order.

This procedure made Mr. Jones feel that he was not really the Purchasing Agent for the Company, but simply a senior clerk. He felt that he had the necessary experience and qualifications to be the Purchasing Agent in the fullest sense of the word. In addition, he knew he was well-respected and held in high esteem by the senior administrative officials within the Company. Furthermore, the supply houses, manufacturers, printers and various other commercial trades with whom he dealt in everyday business, had a high regard for him and sympathized with him for the secondary position in which he found himself with regard to purchasing. This secondary position irritated Mr. Jones. The sales representatives of companies, in trying to sell their products to the Company, would pay a courtesy call to the Purchasing Agent and then call to see the Treasurer because they knew that the Treasurer made the final decision. This situation appealed to the Treasurer's ego, and he played along with the practice. In fact, the Treasurer was convinced that he should, in effect, be Purchasing Agent as well as Treasurer on the premise that purchasing was spending money and any money spent should be subject to the approval of the Treasurer.

To make matters worse, Mr. Jones, as Purchasing Agent on paper (i.e. on the organization chart) reported to the Director of the Personnel Branch, a Mr. Black, who was at the same administrative level as the Treasurer. In practice, Mr. Black never took any interest or hand in the matter and was in reality not in charge of purchasing. So Mr. Jones found himself in the time-honoured position of having the responsibility but not the authority for purchasing.

Mr. Jones had the sympathy and support of his working group. They knew what conditions existed and felt that being under the thumb of the Treasurer was not conducive to a happy atmosphere. As a group, they felt they were capable of doing the purchasing, were in fact doing it, and wanted to show the rest of the organization that there was no need to have purchasing orders approved by a "foreign" branch head. They argued that a purchasing budget for each branch was approved yearly by the company and that a further secondary approval at the time of purchase was an unnecessary financial administrative control.

The other branch heads in the organization had all, at one time or another, objected to the Treasurer's purchase decisions and had indicated that they too were sympathetic to Mr. Jones' predicament. But they had not been sufficiently interested to do anything about it.

Finally, due to the exasperating circumstances in which Mr. Jones found himself, and in order to avoid daily contact and conflict with the Treasurer (who in Jones' opinion was impossible to get along with and often dictatorially refused his recommendations), Jones began placing certain orders—ones which he knew had the approval of branch heads—without the Treasurer's prior approval.

When Mr. Jones began making the purchases of his own, the Treasurer was at first unaware of his actions, and when after a time he began to suspect what was going on, he decided not to make an immediate issue of the matter. At the end of the budget year he found—as he had expected—that several of the branches had overspent their budget allocations. He also felt that they were overstocked and the recipients of a number of unnecessary purchases. He therefore decided to bring the whole issue before the President.

5

The Vague Purchasing Assignment

The Department of Works and Purchasing in a provincial government was established to perform the dual functions of constructing and maintaining public buildings and making centralized purchases of furniture and office supplies required by the civil service.

The first of these functions was carried out adequately over the years but the second function was neglected. Successive deputy ministers, all of whom had been engineers, became so engrossed in the construction and care of buildings that they had little time or personnel available for the task of "providing desks and pencils" to civil servants. Moreover, most of the Department's ministers had been of mediocre ability and had been unwilling to press for substantial funds for purchasing because the legislature always approved such estimates with reluctance. As a result, the purchasing function of the Department remained small and restricted. In the meantime, the departments had begun to do much of their own purchasing, had recruited and trained purchasing staff and had built up separate purchasing sections within their departments.

Then, George Hanson was appointed as the new deputy minister of the Department. Under his leadership, the functions of the Department were redefined, the number of employees was considerably increased and salaries were raised. At the lower levels of the Department, well-qualified personnel was recruited and a training program was established. At the senior level, Mr. Hanson took on the responsibility of making all important decisions himself and even became actively involved in many routine management and personnel matters.

Three years later, a new branch was created in the Department to take over the function of central purchasing of furniture and office supplies for the civil service. Since there was not room in the Departmental building, the new branch had to be located in a new building some distance away. Jim Chambers, one of the new men recruited by Hanson, was put in charge of the new branch over the heads of senior staff. Chambers had no training or experience in the area of large-scale purchasing but he had a reputation as a capable administrator. He was given a free hand to organize the branch and was given the staff he requested. He also obtained expensive modern business equipment and studied the latest methods of purchasing used in the United States. He was not, however, given any terms of reference and the relations of his branch with his own Department and with other departments were not defined. Indeed, while the branch was being set up, Hanson was out of town much of the time. The assistant deputy minister, who was left in control, was preparing to retire. He seldom made any decisions and was very reluctant to provide any guidance.

The new branch developed slowly but appeared to prosper. It began taking over peripheral areas of purchasing which had not been claimed by other departments, such as the purchase of microfilm cameras, readers, contact duplicators and other specialized office equipment. Chambers soon realized that there would be some resistance from other departments to efforts by the branch to move into areas controlled by the purchasing sections of these departments. This meant that the greatest value of centralized purchasing, the economy of buying items in bulk, would not be achieved to the extent he had anticipated. Most departments were unwilling to supply the information required for planned purchasing. Three departments co-operated fully but most preferred to continue in the old manner. Yet, very few departments had enough interest in purchasing to use modern methods and their operations were clearly uneconomical.

Hanson was a very busy man and Chambers had little opportunity to discuss the work of the branch with him. Moreover, since Hanson did not seem very interested in Chambers' activities, Chambers was hesitant to approach him with his hopes and plans for the branch. When the occasion arose, Chambers did mention to Hanson that relations between his branch and other departments required clarification but Hanson simply said that it was too early to take any action in this regard. He rejected Chambers' suggestion that the Cabinet or Treasury Board define the status of central purchasing in the near future because he believed that the departments must be educated first as to the benefits of central purchasing. During the second and third years of the branch's operations, Chambers accompanied his annual reports to Hanson with memos urging more central purchasing in government but he received no reply. In the meantime, Chambers did his best to co-operate with the departments. He joined the Purchasing Officers Association and was appointed to its executive body; he had many officers of the various departments visit his branch; and he gave whatever advice he could.

Then the Department appointed an administrative officer, Victor McLeod, a very capable man with some experience in purchasing, to act as the Departmental administrative and personnel officer under Hanson. McLeod was chosen partly because he had purchasing experience. Two of his former colleagues who followed him to the Department were classified as administrative officers even though their former duties had been primarily in the purchasing area. Hanson asked these two administrative officers to undertake special purchasing assignments with respect to photographic and duplicating equipment. They soon became known as the photography section and Chambers realized that they would be doing all the purchasing of photographic and duplicating equipment without any reference to his staff. Chambers informed Hanson and McLeod that this division of the purchasing function within the Department would make it even more difficult to sell his branch's services to other departments. His communication with Hanson was in the form of a memo and he received no reply.

Soon after Hanson left for a four-month period to study public works in other countries, Chambers learned that a large purchasing assignment involving furniture for a new government building was being handled by a division in the Works Branch of the Department. He also learned that this was being done on orders from Hanson. Chambers was furious and threatened to resign. Immediately upon Hanson's return, Chambers requested an interview but Hanson was so busy that the interview was delayed.

Chambers waited two months and then sent a strongly worded memo to Hanson. He argued that the scattering over several units of the Department of what he regarded as the proper functions of his branch left no clear line of communication regarding purchasing between the Department and other departments. He contended also that this situation made it very difficult for his branch to give the type of service that would induce other departments to rely on the branch for their purchasing. His main request was that the role of the branch be defined in writing and that the scope of its activity be clearly defined.

This memo received a response. Hanson called a meeting to discuss the functions of the Purchasing Branch. The meeting was attended by Hanson, his assistant deputy minister, two division heads from the Works Branch, McLeod and Chambers. Hanson opened the meeting by criticizing the language of the memo and finding minor faults with some of the facts presented. He tried to evade the main issue entirely but Chambers made it clear that he was determined to have the matter cleared up or to resign. Hanson then asked Chambers to submit for approval a statement of the functions of the Purchasing Branch. He also conceded that the Works Branch should define in writing its role in purchasing. Hanson also held out hope that some action would be taken through Treasury Board to clarify and regulate all purchasing activities in the government.

After the meeting, Chambers had a long chat with McLeod who worked very closely with Hanson. Chambers said that Hanson's attitude puzzled him. Hanson seemed to have little confidence in him and in his branch and yet Chambers' annual performance ratings were very high. Although these ratings were made by the assistant deputy minister, the ratings were undoubtedly approved by Hanson. McLeod assured Chambers that there was no loss of confidence and that Hanson preferred to work in this particular manner. He liked to assign jobs to individuals or to sections if he felt they were specially qualified to undertake a specific assignment. To be able to make this division of labour, Hanson himself read through most of the departmental correspondence. The result of Hanson's management style was that an employee was sometimes asked to take on jobs which appeared to be in another person's area of responsibility. Moreover, Hanson was opposed to defining an organization of duties in writing because he wanted to retain flexibility. McLeod pointed out that Hanson had enjoyed a successful career in another province by using these practices.

Chambers carefully wrote out a statement of the functions of his branch as he believed they should be and sent this statement to Hanson. He received no acknowledgement and no answer from Hanson's office. When Chambers called this situation to Hanson's attention several months later, Hanson said that he had been very busy.

In the meantime, monthly progress reports showed that the work of the Purchasing Branch was not increasing in scope. Seventy-five percent of the purchasing was still being done directly by departments. In Chambers' opinion, this system resulted in a great deal of unnecessary overlapping, duplication and inefficiency. Indeed, officers of the Treasury Board's staff were beginning to point out to Chambers that they had expected better results from his branch in regard to increased centralization of purchasing.

Then Chambers was notified by McLeod that his position was going to be reclassified at a higher salary range and that he would be promoted to the reclassified position. Chambers wondered what he should do next.

6

The Successful Leader

Harvey Richmond is a self-confident, energetic and ambitious man who expresses his views in a forceful and persuasive manner. These personal characteristics helped him to be promoted quickly to positions of increasing responsibility in the Research Division of a provincial government department. This Division employed thirty research scientists and engineers, eighteen senior technicians and a support staff of forty-five persons in technical, clerical and secretarial positions.

Shortly after Richmond joined this Division, he was appointed as the head of a large group responsible for providing engineering services to the rest of the Division. The group was composed of three engineers other than Richmond, eight technicians and sixteen support personnel. Richmond rapidly transformed a poorly organized and ineffectual group into a well-managed and highly effective unit which thrived on tight schedules and heavy demands. The group quickly earned a reputation for being able to deliver almost anything the research scientists required.

Gerald Payton, the head of the section containing Richmond's group, was impressed by Richmond's performance and groomed Richmond to succeed him as section head. Richmond's main competition for this position came from John Delaney who led the other group in the section. This group was responsible for basic research and consisted of highly qualified scientists who required very little direction. Indeed, Delaney himself was more interested in scientific matters than in management. When Payton became Director of the Division, Richmond was promoted to the position of section head.

Richmond retained close control over his old group and over Thomas Percy, the new group leader. Percy was not given the authority to run his group and he became in effect a staff officer for Richmond. The performance of the group remained at the same high level it had achieved when Richmond was its head.

The personnel in Delaney's group did not react favourably to the close supervision and the sense of urgency which Richmond imposed on them. Richmond showed little understanding of, or tolerance for, basic research. If he could not see an obvious and early application for a specific research project, that project had little chance of being funded in the next year's budget. Initiative and creativity virtually disappeared in the research group and employee morale declined severely during the four years when Richmond was section head.

By concentrating on applications which exploited the previous work of the research group, Richmond developed an enviable reputation among the senior managers who received most of their feedback from satisfied customers of the section throughout the department. Very few people were surprised when Richmond succeeded Payton as Director of the Division with little competition from the heads of the two other research sections. Percy moved into Richmond's former position but, on Richmond's recommendation, Percy was appointed as *acting* section head.

As Director, Richmond retained the management style which had proved so effective. He had an extraordinary capacity for work and an exceptional memory and he tried to supervise all his professional staff as closely as he had in the past. Moreover, since Percy had not had authority to run the service group and had not been groomed for additional management responsibilities, he was unable to provide effective support to Richmond as acting section head. Thus, Richmond continued to run not only his former section but also his original service group.

Richmond then established a form of project management in the other two sections of the Division and required the project leaders to report directly to him. He thereby stripped the existing group leaders of their authority and used the two section heads essentially in a staff capacity. He also tried to redirect the research of these two sections. He was successful with the section whose work was similar to that of his old section, now headed by Renfrew, but he was unsuccessful with the other section.

Richmond now exercised direct control over a large number of employees. However, several projects began to fall behind schedule as the scientists waited for direction. Little basic research was undertaken. Morale declined in several units of the Division. It seemed that nobody wanted to move without being told.

As a result of his influence with senior management, Richmond then achieved a reorganization in the department whereby he gave up the research section whose work he was unable to redirect and he received from another division a section whose staff had expertise similar to that of his old section. He also received two experienced section heads, Jim Cullen and Bob Fleming. Both men had good reputations as effective managers but their styles are different. Cullen is quiet and slow to speak but confident and forceful when he does speak. Fleming is more impulsive and very outgoing. Percy returned to his former position as group leader and was replaced by Cullen. Fleming became head of the new section.

Along with the staff which Richmond received at the time of the reorganization he also received several ongoing projects, some of which he considered undesirable. Richmond perceived that Fleming would be difficult to control and probably would not accept Richmond's type of management. He gave Fleming responsibility for every project in the Division that was of dubious value or was behind schedule or was inadequately staffed. Cullen seemed more favourably disposed to Richmond's management style and he was given responsibility for most of the projects supported by Richmond himself.

Cullen and his section prospered. However, once he learned the detailed requirements of his position, he began to view Richmond's close interest and support as "unwanted interference" and "lack of confidence." Cullen's staff was content to take orders directly from Richmond because they had been conditioned to operate in this way during Richmond's rise in the Division. In the meantime, Richmond gave Fleming very little support, excessive duties and constant criticism. Fleming arranged to be transferred to another division. Percy, with some reluctance, succeeded Fleming and this time he received a formal appointment as section head.

Since Percy was unable to cope with the difficult problems left by Fleming, Cullen found that Richmond expected him to take on more and more of Percy's responsibilities. Richmond acted as if Percy still worked for Cullen. However, the staff in Percy's section had come to the Division from another division as a result of the reorganization. They were confused as to the line of command when they received orders directly from Richmond rather than through Percy. Morale among these people was extremely low. Initiative and creativity among the senior scientific staff virtually disappeared. The Division's concentration on the application of earlier research work had been effective but there was very little of this research work left to be exploited.

Richmond's immediate superior was totally unaware of this situation. In the eyes of senior management, Richmond had throughout his career been a dynamic leader who had "got results." From all outward appearances, the Division was healthy and highly productive. Cullen, on the other hand, was acutely aware of the Division's problems. He was reluctant to discuss these problems with Richmond. He was also hesitant to appeal to Richmond's superiors because Richmond was so well-respected by senior management. Then Cullen, an ambitious man, learned that Richmond was being promoted to a position in another department. He also learned that he would soon be offered the position of Director of the Division.

7

B And B Or Not

Ronald MacNeil, deputy minister of a federal government department, is retiring. Two years earlier, Dr. MacNeil reached the normal retirement age of 65. He had hoped to retire on schedule because his wife was in ill health, but being a loyal civil servant he agreed to his minister's request that his retirement be deferred first one, then two years. Now he insists, and his minister agrees, that there will be no further deferments.

Dr. MacNeil joined the government of Canada in 1940 after a brilliant career as a researcher in the area of food products. (He received his Ph.D. from Macdonald College of McGill University at the age of 25.) He earned recognition as an administrator during World War II when he created the K-Ration Corporation—a special government agency which devised the food ration kit carried by Canadian infantry during the last years of the war. He seemed to be a logical choice for deputy minister of the new Department of Consumer Affairs when it was created in 1946, and he proved to be a good man as his department grew from 500 to 2,500 personnel over the next 15 years.

Now Dr. MacNeil is regarded by some as being slightly out of step with the times. Most of the programs that have been developed by his department over the years have been federally financed and federally controlled but administered by the provinces. Dr. MacNeil is believed to be against Quebec's insistence that it take over the operation of these programs, and he has been heard to say that he is a bit suspicious of those foreigners from Quebec who can't pronounce the Queen's English properly.

Dr. MacNeil's philosophy of administration is that as much responsibility as possible should be delegated to others. He likes to keep his desk clean and himself available for consultation. He has seen to it that Dr. Arthur Ronson, a man with a background similar to his own, has been groomed to take over from him. Dr. Ronson is 48. Just five years ago Dr. MacNeil appointed Dr. Ronson assistant deputy and director of the department's consumer research division, a division that originally co-ordinated research findings of other government agencies and of the department's research division. Dr. Ronson gradually added staff and boosted his divisional budget until now much of the consumer research is being done by his own staff. His budget has risen in five years from $700,000 to $3.2 million annually. Some of his critics call him an "empire builder", but his own staff are very loyal and regard him as something of a miracle-man because of his ability to supply them constantly with increased personnel and physical resources.

The minister does not completely share Dr. MacNeil's enthusiasm for Dr. Ronson. He is satisfied that Dr. Ronson gets along well with his own staff and that he has good educational qualifications. (Like Dr. MacNeil, Dr. Ronson is a Ph.D. from Macdonald.) He feels, however, that Dr. Ronson is too closely connected to one section of the department, and he is worried by the fact that Dr. Ronson was an outspoken opponent in cabinet committee of the move to turn over consumer products inspection work to Quebec under an opting-out arrangement. One or two other ministers mentioned that while they respect Dr. Ronson for his honesty and his outspoken views, they think he is somewhat out of tune with the times.

The minister mentioned these doubts to Dr. MacNeil who argued that Dr. Ronson's major asset is his willingness to give forthright, honest advice. He pointed out that the Quebec program went ahead despite Dr. Ronson's objections, and in fact, that one or two of the difficulties foreseen by the assistant deputy did develop. It appears that Quebec took over the program before it had the staff available to do a proper job, and there had been one or two annoying incidents which received considerable publicity in the press.

The minister was not fully convinced by these arguments and decided to look elsewhere for a new deputy. Three candidates were turned up by this search.

First, the minister was urged by a senior French-Canadian cabinet colleague—a man whom he respected very highly—to appoint as deputy Gerald Leclerc, age 58, a man two levels down in the department. Dr. Leclerc is a genial man, a Laval graduate, who maintains excellent contacts with Quebec. In fact, he is a director of the Consumer Scientists Association of Quebec, a body that contains among its executive members all the important Quebec administrators. Dr. Leclerc, of course, is also bilingual. The minister had never previously considered him as a deputy candidate, and personnel ratings indicated that his success was due more to his social accomplishments than to administrative competence, but the minister was impressed by the strong recommendation of his senior cabinet colleague. He realized that he need not ask Dr. MacNeil's opinion for he knew that, in Dr. MacNeil's view, Dr. Leclerc's only obvious qualification is the fact that he is the department's senior French-Canadian.

A second possible candidate is the assistant deputy of another department, the Department of Agriculture. This man, Wilfred Robertson, is regarded by many as deputy material. He was passed over in his own department because the new minister, a French-Canadian, wanted a French-speaking deputy. At age 59, one year away from the optional retirement age, Dr. Robertson has decided that he is about ready to quit the civil service. The prime minister learned of this possibility and, quite upset, suggested to the minister of consumer affairs that he should investigate Dr. Robertson as a possible deputy.

The minister scheduled an interview with Dr. Robertson and was impressed. Despite his personal experience, Dr. Robertson spoke sympathetically about French Canada, but admitted he could not speak French and did not have any direct experience in consumer affairs.

The third candidate was Dr. Murray Redfern, the director of the consumer research school at the University of Manitoba. He is easily the most distinguished man in his field. Dr. MacNeil had often spoken highly of him to the minister, and when the minister mentioned his name as a possible deputy, Dr. MacNeil said that even his protegé Dr. Ronson was a less attractive candidate. The minister immediately commenced negotiations with Dr. Redfern but unfortunately, after some months, Dr. Redfern decided that he did not want the job as deputy. He made this decision when Dr. MacNeil's retirement was just four weeks away.

The minister, now faced with an immediate decision, has learned one more disturbing piece of information. Dr. Ronson has been approached by a private firm and has decided to accept the outside post if he is bypassed and anyone else is made deputy. He would have been willing to serve under Dr. Redfern, but he is not prepared to stay if either Dr. Leclerc or Dr. Robertson is appointed.

8

Fear of Flying

The Commissioner of Official Languages received several complaints between March and December 1975 from air traffic controllers in Quebec City and Montreal and from Quebecair pilots and Quebec government pilots. The essence of these complaints was that the right to use the French language in air traffic control, both for ground-to-air and ground-to-ground communications did not exist in the Province of Quebec.

The Commissioner realized that this matter was not only the most complex one he had ever handled but that it was also a highly technical one involving possible danger to human life. He therefore consulted persons with specialized knowledge of air traffic control who represented a variety of organizations, including the Ministry of Transport (MOT), the International Civil Aviation Organization (ICAO), the Canadian Owners and Pilots Association (COPA), the Canadian Airline Pilots Association (CALPA) and the Canadian Air Traffic Controllers Association (CATCA). He also met with pilots of the Quebec Government Air Service of Quebecair and he visited control towers in Montreal, Quebec City and Paris (Orly and Charles de Gaulle). Later, he had discussions with the newly formed l'Association des Gens de l'Air du Québec. During these consultations, the Commissioner received conflicting opinions as to whether bilingualism would improve or threaten safety in air traffic control. However, the representatives of the national associations emphasized the need for caution in dealing with this matter.

Section 25 of the Official Languages Act requires that the Commissioner "take all actions and measures within his authority with a view to ensuring recognition of the status of each of the official languages and compliance with the spirit and intent of this Act in the administration of the affairs of the institutions of the Parliament and Government of Canada. . . ." (See Appendix I for other relevant sections of the Act.) The Commissioner and his colleagues did not, however, possess the technical knowledge needed to reconcile, in detailed aviation regulations, the requirements of the Act with air safety. Both legally and technically, the Ministry of Transport was the appropriate authority to determine what course of action was in line with the Aeronautics Act. Also, the Commissioner realized that the Official Languages Act, like any other statute, must be implemented with common sense. He therefore considered the relative importance of bilingualism and air safety in terms of the public interest. This meant that the matter of safety must be of prime concern but that the real effect on safety of using one or both of Canada's official languages at certain Canadian airports must be examined carefully.

The Commissioner concluded that the restrictions on the use of French were "contrary to the spirit and intent" of the Official Languages Act" but were in accordance with the provisions of another Act of Parliament," namely the Aeronautics Act. (See section 31 of the Official Languages Act in Appendix 1.)

He therefore recommended in July 1975 that "the Ministry of Transport, continuing its consultations with all interested parties, determine that degree of bilingualism which is compatible with safety in air traffic control, aiming at recognizing as much as possible the equality of the two official languages but always giving overriding priority to the safety of air travellers and aircrew."

And in the interest of promoting air safety, the Commissioner also suggested that the Ministry assess the value of three additional suggestions:

> a) that where bilingual air traffic control services are not available, practical, job-related language courses be offered on a voluntary basis to both unilingual English- and French-speaking pilots in at least Quebec, the National Capital Region, Northern and Eastern New Brunswick and Northern and Eastern Ontario, as well as to personnel in the Advisory Stations in the above-mentioned areas;
> b) that a standard vocabulary in French for air traffic control be developed and distributed as soon as possible;
> c) that uniform tests be administered by the Ministry of Transport or by the Department of Communications to air traffic controllers providing bilingual services, to ensure that they have adequate comprehension in both official languages.

He requested that he be kept informed of all decisions taken in this matter and he assured the Ministry of Transport that he was at its disposal for any further consultation about linguistic matters.

During the months that followed, the Commissioner observed that the issue of bilingualism in air traffic control had become highly politicized. Both English-speaking and French-speaking aviation personnel threatened strikes and exchanged harsh words in public. On September 5, 1975, the Commissioner invited all the parties concerned to a meeting with a view to moving this contentious matter back into the technical area. As a result of this meeting, a committee composed of French-speaking and English-speaking air traffic controllers, airline pilots and MOT personnel was established under the chairmanship of an MOT official. The members of the Committee agreed to four principles suggested by the Commissioner, namely

> 1) To recommend a realistic policy for air-ground communication, taking Canada's linguistic duality into account, while always giving overriding priority to air safety.
> 2) In considering air safety their common and paramount concern, committee members agree to seek an objective technical solution

> without imposing preconceptions or preconditions.
> 3) Recognizing that one or more minority reports would probably defeat the purpose of finding a safe and universally acceptable solution, the committee will try to produce within the shortest possible time a unanimous report for urgent action by the Ministry of Transport.
> 4) While the committee is working, and until a decision on its report is announced, committee members and their delegating organizations would respect a moratorium on all public statements about this subject and on any action or threat of action which might harm the climate of technical and professional objectivity needed to find a solution.

Since the Committee members were apparently unable to adhere to the second principle, the Committee ceased operation in early October. Relations between the contending groups continued to deteriorate.

Then, in early December, the Commissioner became involved in the issue once more. Two French-speaking air traffic controllers based in Montreal were suspended for using French in ground-to-ground communications and an English-speaking controller, also based in Montreal, was given a day's leave of absence without pay for abandoning his position to protest the use of French by his fellow controllers in ground-to-ground communications.

On December 11, the Commissioner wrote to the Deputy Minister of Transport as follows:

> I refer to our letter of December 10, 1975, concerning two air traffic controllers who were suspended at the Dorval Air Traffic Control Centre.
>
> Because of the extreme urgency of the case, I visited the Control Centre last night in order to meet with the complainants and their superiors. As agreed with Mr. Walter McLeish, I was accompanied by Mr. C. G. Foy of your Ministry.
>
> In addition to Messrs. M. Pitre and L. Desmarais, I met with both anglophone and francophone controllers. While consulting with these persons, I realized that finding a "technical" solution which everyone could respect would be impossible unless steps were taken rapidly to improve the psychological atmosphere of the Control Centre. . . .
>
> The discussions I had in Montreal also convinced me that your Ministry, while always giving overriding priority to air safety, will have to find, as quickly as possible, ways to allow the use of the French language in ground-to-ground communications between controllers who wish to use French. While I recognize that your Ministry's undeniable duty, from a legal and moral standpoint, is to protect the public if air safety appears to be in jeopardy, I find it abnormal, in principle, to oblige French-speaking controllers to speak to each other in English in the province of Quebec.
>
> Without wishing for the moment to make formal recommendations which might take me into an area where I do not have your

> competence, I would like to propose for now, as a working hypothesis, a three-point analysis, the essential goal of which is to bring the whole question back to a level where reason will prevail over all other considerations:
> 1) Given the circumstances existing for several weeks at the Dorval Control Centre, the two suspensions seemed inevitable. Even though, in ground-to-ground communications, certain interested parties assess in varying degrees the importance of the purely linguistic factor in air safety, our investigation reveals that the general climate of indiscipline at the Control Centre at the time of the suspension was a very clear threat to air safety.
> 2) The suspended employees (Messrs. S. Cormier and R. Buisson), and their superiors (Messrs. M. Pitre and L. Desmarais), were all to a certain extent victims of a situation which had been allowed to deteriorate for too long; indeed, the suspended persons were working in an atmosphere where insults and provocations between certain anglophones and certain francophones were commonplace: consequently, one can reasonably believe that the thoughtless behaviour of the suspended persons may have been the result of exasperation, tension, as well as perplexity about the often uneven application of sometimes ambiguous directives in the past. These same circumstances obliged the two supervisors to enforce regulations in conditions which, no doubt, were very distressing to them personally and which led them to carry the blame, in a certain part of the press, unjustly in my opinion, for having taken an unpopular decision.
> 3) Since the Ministry will announce today that it will be in a position, at the beginning of January, to evaluate a study now in progress which seems to offer serious hope that French may be used in certain ground-to-ground communications, it might find it useful to consider softening the financial effects of the two sanctions as a freely decided gesture to lower tensions. In my view, such a gesture would constitute neither a defeat nor a victory for anyone, nor would it give other employees a licence to commit acts of indiscipline affecting air safety while a solution is being worked out in short order.
>
> Indeed, even though my mandate is to defend linguistic equality, I consider that the safety of passengers and aircrew must not in the slightest way be jeopardized by any political consideration. The problem now is simply to find a realistic procedure allowing us, if only briefly, to take the politics out of an issue that in the final analysis is technical in nature and, in my opinion, must be settled on technical grounds. At bottom, all the interested parties, be they Anglophones or Francophones, controllers, pilots or departmental specialists, state that their attitudes on language use are based solely on concern for air safety. I believe that Canadians expect all these professionals to explain the soundness of their respective positions through objective arguments. Plainly, this will be possible only if the Ministry manages to establish the climate of serenity which is one of the principal goals of the steps we have taken and of the present letter.

And on December 12, the Commissioner sent another letter to the Deputy Minister which said in part that

> In conjunction with our investigation already in progress concerning language procedures in ground-to-ground communications at the Dorval Air Traffic Control Centre, I would like to specify that the suggestion I made in my letter of December 11, 1975 concerning the softening of the financial effects of the two suspensions also applies to the English-speaking controller who had to take a day's leave without pay.

The Ministry responded to these letters by sending the Commissioner a press release dated December 13 and entitled: "Transport Minister Otto Lang Announces Bilingual Air Communications Will Be Introduced Progressively in Quebec." In the press release, the Minister announced that air radio operators in Quebec were being "authorized to provide advisory services in the French language" whenever this practice would be in the interest of safety. (Air radio operators provide information on weather and flight clearance to pilots.) French-language lexicons, instruction manuals and notices to airmen would be prepared and distributed by April 1, 1976, and the language capabilities of the radio operators would be certified. As of April 1, 1976, all flight and airport advisory services would be provided by air radio operators in French as well as in English.

At Bagotville, Canadian Armed Forces air traffic controllers with a knowledge of French were authorized to begin at once to use French in civil VFR (Visual Flight Rules) Operations but not in IFR (Instrument Flight Rules) Operations.

The Minister also announced that in early February, 1976 the aviation associations and the aviation industry would be invited to participate in experiments and demonstrations on the new Air Traffic Control Electronic Simulator in order to develop procedures which would permit the introduction of bilingual communications in IFR operations in Quebec, while taking account of safety requirements. The last stage in the implementation of bilingual air-ground communications would be the introduction of these communications in VFR operations in the terminal areas of Dorval and Mirabel, but only after appropriate procedures for IFR operations in Quebec had been successfully developed and introduced.

The Minister also followed the Commissioner's suggestion that the financial loss to the two French-speaking controllers who were suspended and the English-speaking controller who was given a one-day leave without pay be reduced.

The Commissioner informed the complainants of the results of his investigation and closed the files.

During the next six months, the dispute over the effect of bilingual air traffic control on air safety became more intense and more complicated. Relations worsened between English-speaking and French-speaking controllers and pilots and between the leaders of CATCA and CALPA on one side and the government on the other. Then, on June 20, the air line pilots began a national strike in opposition to the government's policy on bilingual air traffic control.

Public opinion was divided on the issue. On June 25, the Prime Minister said that the dispute was Canada's most serious crisis since the conscription crisis of the Second World War. On June 26, the Minister of Transport said that "the leaders of the controllers are not opponents of bilingualism, but are being used by those who are . . . . There is no evidence that there is a greater proportion of opponents to the national bilingual policy within the controllers and pilots organizations than in the country as a whole."

The strike ended on June 28 after the Minister of Transport reached an agreement on behalf of the government with CALPA and CATCA. The end of the strike ensured that there would be no disruption of air traffic during the Olympic games which began two weeks later. The agreement provided, among other things, for the appointment of a commission of inquiry to evaluate the safety implications of bilingual air traffic control. A French-speaking Cabinet Minister who resigned from the Cabinet over the terms of the agreement, said that he could "not stay in a government that is prepared to negotiate bilingualism." The Minister of Transport assured officials of l'Association des Gens de l'Air, who were unhappy with the agreement, that there was "no move by this government away from our fundamental commitment to bilingualism." The Director of Air Traffic Control for the Ministry of Transport was reported to have said that "two languages are perhaps less convenient, but certainly not less safe."

On June 29, the Commissioner of Official Languages appeared on a CBC television program. He was quoted in the press as having said, with respect to bilingualism in general, that the government had done a "crummy job" of communicating what he described as "overdue fair play" for bilingualism in Canada.

Appendix I
The Official Languages Act

25. It is the duty of the Commissioner to take all actions and measures within his authority with a view to ensuring recognition of the status of each of the official languages and compliance with the spirit and intent of this Act in the administration of the affairs of the institutions of the Parliament and Government of Canada and, for that purpose, to conduct and carry out investigations either on his own initiative or pursuant to any complaint made to him and to report and make recommendations with respect thereto as provided in this Act.

26. (1) Subject to this Act, the Commissioner shall investigate any complaint made to him to the effect that, in any particular instance or case,

(a) the status of an official language was not or is not being recognized, or

(b) the spirit and intent of this Act was not or is not being complied with

in the administration of the affairs of any of the institutions of the Parliament or Government of Canada.

(2) A complaint may be made to the Commissioner by any person or group of persons, whether or not they speak or represent a group speaking the official language the status or use of which is at issue.

(3) If in the course of investigating any complaint it appears to the Commissioner that, having regard to all the circumstances of the case, any further investigation is unnecessary, he may in his discretion refuse to investigate the matter further.

(4) The Commissioner may, in his discretion, refuse to investigate or cease to investigate any complaint if in his opinion

(a) the subject matter of the complaint is trivial,

(b) the complaint is frivolous or vexatious or is not made in good faith, or

(c) the subject matter of the complaint does not involve a contravention or failure to comply with the spirit and intent of this Act, or does not for any other reason come within his authority under this Act.

(5) Where the Commissioner decides to refuse to investigate or cease to investigate any complaint, he shall inform the complainant of his decision and shall give his reasons therefor. . . .

30. The Commissioner has, in relation to the carrying out of any investigation under this Act, power

(a) to summon and enforce the attendance of witnesses and compel them to give oral or written evidence on oath, and to produce such documents and things as the Commissioner deems requisite to the full investigation and consideration of any matter within his authority under this Act, in the same manner and to the same extent as a superior court of record;

(b) to administer oaths;

(c) to receive and accept such evidence and other information whether on oath or by affidavit or otherwise as in his discretion he sees fit, whether or not such evidence or information is or would be admissible in a court of law; and

(d) subject to such limitations as the Governor in Council in the interests of defence or security may prescribe, to enter any premises occupied by any department or other institution of the Parliament

or Government of Canada and carry out therein such inquiries within his authority under this Act as he sees fit.

31. (1) This section applies where, after carrying out any investigation under this Act, the Commissioner is of the opinion that an act or omission that was the subject of the investigation is or was or appears to be or have been

(a) contrary to the provisions of this Act;

(b) contrary to the spirit and intent of this Act but in accordance with the provisions of any other Act of the Parliament of Canada or any regulations thereunder, or in accordance with a practice that leads or is likely to lead to any involuntary contravention of this Act; or

(c) based wholly or partly on mistake or inadvertence.

(2) Where the Commissioner is of opinion

(a) that the act or omission that was the subject of the investigation should be referred to any department or other institution concerned for consideration and action if necessary,

(b) that any Act or regulations thereunder described in paragraph *(b)* of subsection (1) should be considered or any practice described in that paragraph should be altered or discontinued, or

(c) that any other action should be taken,

the Commissioner shall report his opinion and his reasons therefor to the Clerk of the Privy Council and the deputy head or other administrative head of any department or other institution concerned and may in his report make such recommendations with respect thereto as he thinks fit, and, in any such case, may request the department or other institution concerned to notify him within a specified time of the action, if any, that it proposes to take to give effect to his recommendations.

9
This Hour Has Seven Days

In 1964, two experienced producers of the CBC, Douglas Leiterman and Patrick Watson, conceived a new magazine-type CBC public affairs television show to fit into the prime viewing time at 10 p.m. Sunday evenings after the *Ed Sullivan Show* and *Bonanza.* In their presentation to CBC management, they said, "We propose a new kind of journalism, which will bring public affairs to ordinary citizens . . . ." The idea was accepted by the management and a new program known as *This Hour Has Seven Days* went on the air in the fall of 1964, with Mr. Leiterman and Mr. Watson as co-producers and John Drainie as host.

Almost immediately, *Seven Days* became involved in controversy. Senior officers in the corporation objected to some of the more sensational productions, and some of the rebukes and the producers' justifications reached the press instead of remaining within the CBC. Management criticized the producers for airing a prolonged interview with George Lincoln Rockwell, the head of the Nazi Party in the United States, and vetoed the plan to air a segment of a film about the prime minister, Mr. Pearson, which the corporation had earlier banned in its entirety. One of the top officials, H. G. Walker, general manager of the English network, objected to a satire on the existence of God. The management objected to another sequence showing an interview filmed with Fred Fawcett, an inmate at Penetanguishene. The *Seven Days* crew, carrying a concealed camera in a picnic basket, got in to see Mr. Fawcett by accompanying his sister.

Management also became involved when a *Seven Days* camera crew went to the home of a former cabinet minister, the Hon. Pierre Sevigny, and managed to obtain film showing Larry Zolf, a reporter, being bonked over the head by Mr. Sevigny's cane. *Seven Days* producers decided not to air the film immediately but decided to use it a week after the incident; management then stepped in and overruled the decision. Finally, management stepped in when the program's hot-seat interviewing technique caused a great deal of controversy; a round-table discussion approach was introduced for a number of the programs to make the interviews seem less abusive.

The normal method of control by CBC management is to give rough guidelines to a show and then allow a producer the freedom he desires, but to reserve the right to act in a *post facto* manner and veto a project after it is completed, or to criticize a program after it is aired. This seemed to be the only way that CBC management could control the creative talent of the *Seven Days* crew. Management's general position was that it liked the basic format and idea of *Seven Days* but wanted it toned down from its original controversial form. Roy Faibish, the Ottawa producer of *Seven Days,* said that management wanted "the status, prestige and glory without the agony".

Most of the employees on a big show like *Seven Days* are not salaried staff with tenure but are under contract with the CBC. These contracts are normally negotiated and renewed on an annual basis. Long-term employees have every reason to expect that their contracts will be renewed; nevertheless, this is a form of control that management has over producers and other creative employees.

The disputes between the show's producers and the management led to the inevitable strains. After the first season, host John Drainie retired from the show and Mr. Leiterman became the sole executive producer. Mr. Watson gave up his role as co-producer to become co-host with a McGill University professor, Laurier LaPierre. However, Mr. Watson continued as executive producer of the *Document* series which was produced along with *Seven Days* and periodically filled the 10 p.m. Sunday time slot. One of the *Document* series, "The Mills of the Gods", a film on Viet-Nam produced by Beryl Fox, won several awards in the United States.

The producers of *Seven Days* achieved a maximum impact on the public; nearly every English-speaking Canadian got a glimpse of *Seven Days,* and the Sunday night audience reached proportions never before achieved by public affairs television in Canada. The show used its weekly budget of $37,000 to gain an audience of over 3,000,000, an all-time high.

To understand exactly what happened in the spring of 1966 it is necessary to understand the administrative structure of the CBC, which is a bit complicated. At the top of the CBC, a crown corporation, is the board of directors which includes the president and vice-president—at the time of the show Messrs. Alphonse Ouimet and W. E. S. Briggs. Line Management extends down into network broadcasting, English division, with Mr. H. G. Walker as vice-president and general manager. Under Mr. Walker is the Assistant General Manager and the News and Public Affairs operation, and under this is Mr. Reeves Haggan who is public affairs general supervisor. Public affairs itself is divided up into a number of units; one of these was *Seven Days.* Serving as liaison between *Seven Days,* its general supervisor and other public affairs units was Mr. Hugh Gauntlett. The producer, Doug Leiterman, was responsible for putting on the show within the budget allotted to him.

In early 1966, according to information made public later, Mr. Walker and CBC management admired and respected Mr. Leiterman's ability and wanted to retain the basic format of *Seven Days;* however, management also felt that Mr. Leiterman and Mr. Watson were too strong as a team and were building up a "little empire" within the corporation. Management thought that it was wasteful to use two top public affairs producers on the same show.

On April 5, 1966, Mr. Haggan, the public affairs supervisor, was told by Mr. Walker that management had decided not to renew the contracts of Mr. Watson and Mr. LaPierre as co-hosts on *Seven Days*. The stories of management and *Seven Days* staff diverge here. The CBC claims that at this stage Mr. Watson was slated to organize and produce a two-language centennial series called *Quarterly Report*. The other story is that *Quarterly Report* was not created until later and was used by management as a rationalization after the event. Evidently, Mr. Haggan was not told of the *Quarterly Report* idea at this discussion. Mr. Haggan asked for time to consider the implications of the move and left (so he said later) assuming that no immediate contact would be made with Mr. Watson or Mr. LaPierre.

The following day, April 6, Mr. Walker called Mr. Watson and told him that his contract and the contract of his co-host, Laurier LaPierre, would not be renewed for the following year. Mr. Watson said later he listened to Mr. Walker with "amazement, disbelief and with a sense of controlled fury". Mr. Walker, describing the conversation, said it was "completely affable, friendly, useful . . . we parted with a handshake". Evidently management was anxious to retain Mr. Watson's services, but, if an offer was made, the terms were unacceptable. Mr. Watson immediately telephoned Mr. Leiterman, his executive producer, who was vacationing in Florida at the time.

The editorial board of *Seven Days,* which included Mr. Watson and Mr. Leiterman, then decided not to tell Mr. LaPierre of the decision for they agreed that the problem might be solved internally through discussion with top management, that is, with Mr. Walker and perhaps even with the president, Mr. Ouimet. Mr. Haggan, acting independently, sent a memo directly to Mr. Ouimet, complaining about the decision to drop Mr. Watson from *Seven Days* without going through him in the normal line of command. It is not clear what discussions were held but by April 15th, just over a week later, the editorial board of *Seven Days* realized that management would stand firm in its decision. Mr. Leiterman then informed Mr. LaPierre that his contract would not be renewed. The story broke in the newspapers the same day and the decision not to renew the contracts of the *Seven Days* personnel became a major public controversy. The Secretary of State, Hon. Judy LaMarsh, who reported to Parliament for the CBC, said the explosion between management and the creative personnel had been coming for a long time and described the dispute as the tip of an iceberg, symptomatic of more fundamental problems.

CBC—ORGANIZATION IN MARCH, 1966

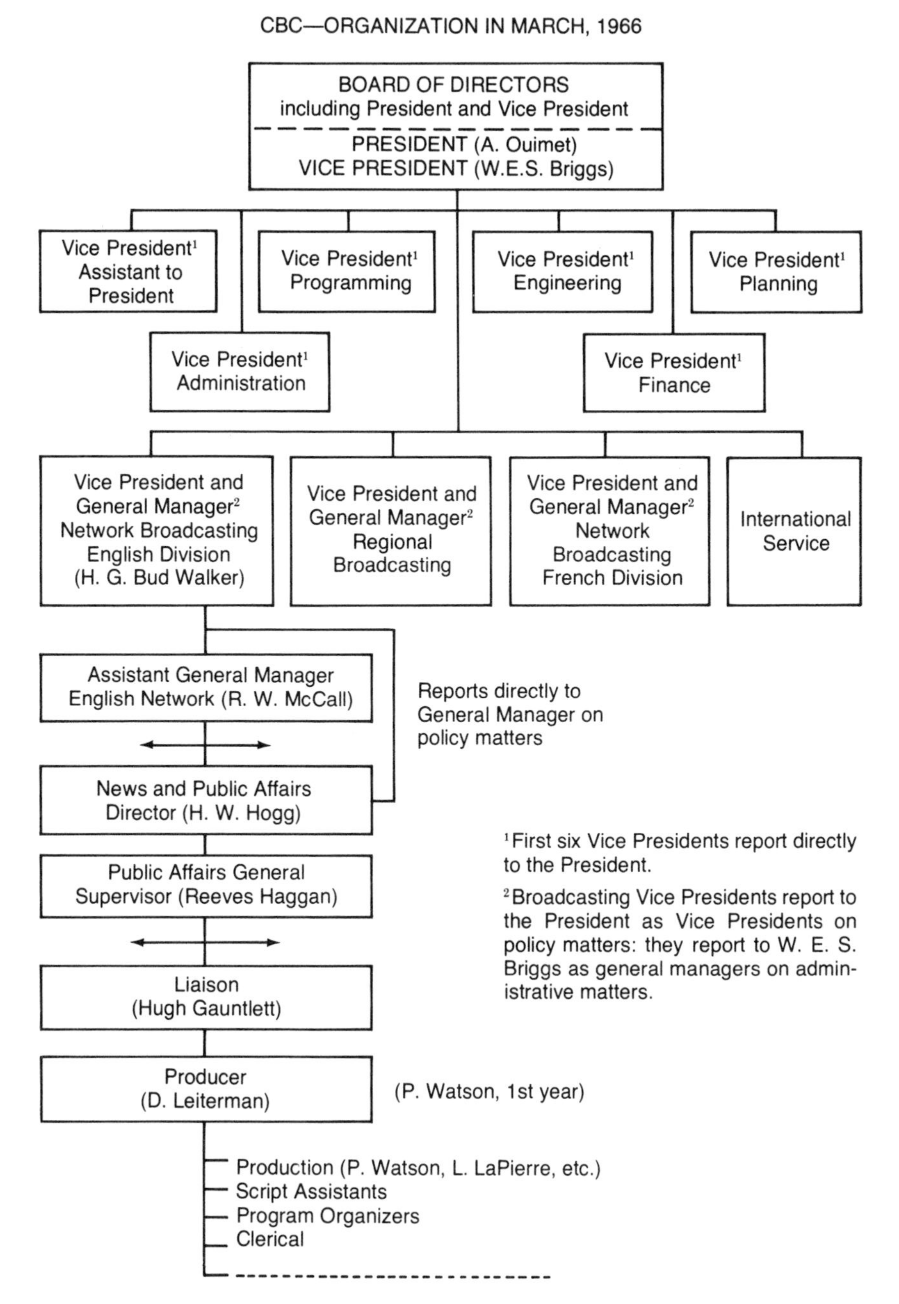

[1] First six Vice Presidents report directly to the President.

[2] Broadcasting Vice Presidents report to the President as Vice Presidents on policy matters: they report to W. E. S. Briggs as general managers on administrative matters.

Note: This organization chart was drawn from oral reports; apparently no complete chart for this period is available.

Members of *Seven Days,* now feeling that management was being untruthful in its version of the dissolution of *Seven Days,* launched a public attack on management: an effort was made to form "save the CBC" committees on university campuses; speeches were made to various groups; and there was a constant flow of information to the press. Mr. Leiterman complained that the basic issue in the dispute was that the proper chain of authority was bypassed by CBC management and that there was no 'mutual confidence' between management and producers. He said that his contract stated that he was given the responsibility for the selection of scripts and principal artists and yet these two artists were going to be dismissed without prior consultation with him. Mr. Watson argued that CBC policies were made in a very awkward way. "In this confusing situation," he said, "we have department supervisors, executive producers and producers being informed of head office decisions by performers." He said that management by reaching over the heads of supervisors to fire him and Mr. LaPierre was destroying confidence and breaking down communication.

(The suggestion that there is a communication problem at the CBC is not a new one. The Fowler Committee in 1964 had said, "It is a paradox that an agency engaged in communications seems to have failed to perfect its internal communications.")

On April 19th, 70 members of the Toronto Producers Association issued an ultimatum to CBC President Alphonse Ouimet and told him the CBC had 24 hours to re-open the case or face drastic measures, if necessary involving the withdrawal of producers' services. On the same day the Commons Committee on Broadcasting, Films and Assistance to the Arts announced that there would be an investigation into the *Seven Days* dispute.

On April 20th, the CBC president, Mr. Ouimet, averted the walkout of producers by agreeing to meet Tom Koch, president of the Toronto Producers Association.

On April 25th, the Toronto Producers Association issued another ultimatum to Mr. Ouimet demanding

- no arbitrary program decisions without prior consultation with the producers concerned,
- no dismissal or discipline of producers without demonstrable cause,
- disputes be arbitrated by a mediator appointed by the federal government.

Mr. Ouimet refused to re-open negotiations on the dismissals. He said the question of the dismissals was a simple one. "Mr. LaPierre . . . has a one-year contract with us as host and we think we can find a better man next year . . . . Mr. Watson is not being moved because he is not a good host—he is a good host—but because he is part of a combination that I have described as giving us a lot of difficulty."

On April 26th, Prime Minister Pearson said the government would be glad to use its "good offices" short of "intervention in the affairs of the CBC" to help settle the dispute. On April 28th, Gerard Pelletier, chairman of the Commons' Committee, recommended to the Prime Minister that he use his good offices to avoid the possibility of any stoppage of CBC services. On April 29th, Mr. Pearson conferred with Mr. Ouimet, and on May 1st, a walkout was averted with the appointment of Stuart Keate, the publisher of the *Vancouver Sun,* as "conciliator". Mr. Keate said he was not a "mediator" in the technical sense of the word since he had "no powers, no authority and was not being paid for his services". He did file an independent and comprehensive review of the *Seven Days* dispute and made comments and suggestions thereon.

The show went on the air for the second time at that point, with the host saying, thanks to the good offices of the Prime Minister, "This Hour *Has* Seven Days."

During the Commons Committee hearings management said that it held fast to its policy of fairness and objectivity, avoidance of bias and partisanship, particularly in news and public affairs, and it did not condone the use of deceit or misrepresentation in obtaining and presenting program material; management made particular reference to the interview with Fred Fawcett in Penetanguishene during which the camera was concealed in a picnic basket and CBC personnel were not identified. Mr. Leiterman defended the segments involving a concealed camera and non-identification of CBC personnel, saying that this was part of the new-journalism and the *"cinéma vérité"* approach, and it was necessary to keep people informed and to make them involved in the program. Television journalism could not be aired without undermining the old myths of objectivity and "studious neutrality". Mr. Ouimet said that one serious shortcoming of the program was its departure from established corporation policy. It was not the policy of the CBC to editorialize; the policy of the CBC was to have the hosts *not* expressing their own opinions. He pointed out that Mr. LaPierre had wiped away a tear after an interview with the parents of Stephen Truscott, a youth who had been convicted of murder. Mr. LaPierre commented, "They decided to fire me in January, and I didn't start to cry until March."

The *Seven Days* dispute ended with most of those involved out of work as far as the CBC was concerned, and with the show itself dropped. Mr. Leiterman was offered a new contract but it contained a clause under which he would have to accept CBC policy procedures and direction. He pointed out that this requirement was already in the standard contract and that to add this as a special rider was tantamount to a formal statement of lack of confidence; he described this as a loyalty oath and refused to sign it and left to join CBS in New York. Mr. Watson took a part-time post at the University of Waterloo. Beryl Fox, who had produced the award winning documentary "Mills of the Gods", left Canada. Roy Faibish, *Seven Days* Ottawa producer, joined the private network CTV. Laurier LaPierre went back to full-time teaching and announced he would be an NDP candidate at the next election. Larry Zolf, the man who was hit on the head with a cane, and Robert Hoyt, a *Seven Days* producer, rejoined the CBC staff and a new show, *Sunday,* was inaugurated as the public affairs successor to *Seven Days*.

10

The Difficult Supervisor

Mr. Ian MacIver, who has been Personnel Counselor for the department for the past three years, recently became interested in the problem of alcoholism. Mr. MacIver's duties involved advising line managers on matters of personnel management and counselling them on difficult problems which they encounter from time to time. He also works with problem employees and gives them advice and help when he can. He has the confidence of management and has been able to help both employees and their superiors.

Working with the Training Division, Mr. MacIver assisted in the organization and implementation of a series of half-day training conferences on alcoholism for all supervisors and administrators in the department. After one of these conferences, Mr. James Weeks, a division chief in "Q" Branch, mentioned that he would like to talk to Mr. MacIver about a staff problem which was giving him some concern, and which might involve alcoholism; he mentioned the name of Mrs. Pansey Laing, one of his supervisors. A meeting was arranged for the following Wednesday.

MacIver took out the personnel file of Mrs. Laing and found the following:

(a) Born in 1929; married 1950; high school education.
 1956—Joined the Department as a junior clerk
 1958—Promoted to senior clerk
 1966—Promoted to Officer Grade 2
 1970—Promoted to Assistant Section Head, at Officer Grade 3 level.
 1972—Transferred to present unit as an Officer Grade 3. File not clear—apparently she had given trouble in her last position.

(b) Beginning about 1961, all her sick leave and vacation leave was used up in a series of short absences, and there seemed to be a pattern of her using more and more leave without pay:

Year	Days L.W.O.P.	Year	Days L.W.O.P.
1964	2	1969	16
1965	7	1970	7
1966	0	1971	12
1967	8	1972	23
1968	11	1973	34

(c) Until 1972, the efficiency ratings were somewhat higher than average and seemed to show nothing of particular significance. In 1972, however, she was rated lower, Below Average. Her recurring absences were noted under WEAK POINTS; also noted was what was called "inability to get along with her staff." The 1973 efficiency rating report was unsatisfactory, and her annual salary increment had been denied.

(d) A careful check of the specific dates showed that of the 68 working days of fiscal 1973-74 which followed a weekend, a holiday or a pay day, Mrs. Laing was absent 47 of them.

Mr. MacIver also dropped in to see Al Gessup, the Chief of Personnel. When Mrs. Laing's name was mentioned, Gessup laughed and remarked, "Boy, you've picked a 'dilly' there. What are you trying to do, Ian, get yourself into trouble?" Gessup explained that the 1971 transfer had been at the request of both Mrs. Laing and the boss, that the psychiatrist at the Health Centre had advised them last year to try "making the best of it with this unfortunate woman," and that they had been having a great deal of trouble in replacing staff who had left her section, especially during the past 18 months. MacIver questioned Gessup specifically on what he meant by "getting into trouble with Mrs. Laing." Gessup told him how Mrs. Laing had telephoned him at his home on several different occasions in connection with her 1971 transfer and had cried, blustered and even threatened him. Apparently she has friends who, she thinks, are influential with the top people.

At the Wednesday meeting Weeks brought along Mr. Stan Hall, the Administrative Officer of "Q" Branch. Weeks started the discussion by summarizing some of the biographical data on Mrs. Laing and then continued by painting a picture of increasing difficulties. For weeks at a time Mrs. Laing appeared quite capable and up to her former standard, but then she would stay away and come back aggressive, incapable and sometimes distraught. He had talked to her a number of times and had warned her but this didn't do any good. When he was really stern, as on the last rating, she would start crying. Mr. MacIver asked whether Mrs. Laing's difficulties were due to drinking. Hall answered: "I'm not sure that girl is an alcoholic. I'm not even sure she is what you call a problem drinker. I know she is a heavy drinker." Weeks gave MacIver the impression that he was convinced drinking was involved with much of Mrs. Laing's trouble; he was not, however, very positive about it. He admitted that he had never caught her drinking on the job, but was fairly sure that she drank every noon hour. He maintained that whenever she was absent on pay day (which was often), she always came in for her cheque—usually without letting him know about it.

When MacIver enquired about Mrs. Laing's competence as an assistant supervisor, both Weeks and Hall assured him that she had been clever, technically competent, and, until a little over a year ago, resourceful and even creative. She had never, however, been very competent as a supervisor of others. She was sarcastic, disagreeable and too certain that she was always right. Mr. MacIver then asked whether, in their opinion, Mrs. Laing earned her salary even when she was on the job. They both agreed that in the last year she did not. The two main difficulties were that she used a great deal of her own and other people's time in talking about her troubles, and that, being away so much and not knowing the current work, she would bother Miss Burns or one of the senior clerks in getting up to date.

Hall went on to say that Pansey Laing was "certainly no asset as far as publicity goes." He repeated several 'incidents' that he had heard about Mrs. Laing, and one that he knew about first-hand. He left no doubt that he considered Mrs. Laing to have few moral principles. MacIver asked about any documentation that might be available, but Hall admitted that there was none.

MacIver then asked if they would like him to arrange to have a member of Alcoholics Anonymous meet with Mrs. Laing, Mr. Weeks and himself. Mr. Weeks appeared to like the idea at first. Mr. Hall, however, was very much against it. "It isn't very wise," he said, "to go calling this woman an alcoholic; we can't prove it you know. And besides, having her meet an A.A. man, and hinting about her drinking—boy, she'd hit the roof! By the way, did you know that I discussed this woman with our Director? He told me to be sure of proof before I took any action; he even intimated that he thought we might be conducting a witch hunt."

As he walked away from the meeting, Ian MacIver considered various courses of action he might take; first, he decided to see his own superior, Mr. A. Hope.

When he mentioned Mrs. Laing's name to Mr. Hope, the Director became very serious: 'Yes . . . yes, I have known Pansey Laing for almost 20 years now. Al and one of the other Personnel Officers have, I know, for the past year or so, considered her to be something of a problem. Personally, I think that they are only seeing one side of this unfortunate woman. Oh, she is a bit of a rough diamond, but her heart is in the right place. Back in the 60's when we were reorganizing, Pansey Laing was one of our most reliable people—she was indispensable, a real workhorse! Her husband is not well, you know. He hasn't worked for three or four years; he is a professional man of some kind—or was. Looking after a 'crotchety' invalid doesn't bring out the best side of anybody." Mr. Hope went on to tell how Mrs. Laing had come to him only last week and how sorry he had been for her. "I consider Mrs. Laing," Mr. Hope said, with some conviction, "to be one of those people who, after years of good service, have lost ground through no fault of their own. I believe that this Department has a definite responsibility toward this poor woman."

11

The Health of Mr. Cole

"It's my opinion that this fellow should be dismissed," said Mr. McCoy. Mr. Connor stirred restlessly in his chair and then replied: "I always find it difficult to make a decision in this kind of case but I am willing to support your recommendation."

Mr. McCoy was the Administrative Officer in the Vancouver office of the Health Protection Branch of the Department of National Health and Welfare. Mr. Connor was the District Director of the Branch. The major responsibility of the Vancouver office and of other field offices of the Branch is to enforce Branch programs at the field level by inspecting food and drug manufacturing and distribution plants and by monitoring recalls by manufacturers.

The two men were discussing the case of Mr. N. E. Cole who had been an employee in the Branch for eight years. He had been appointed as an inspection officer with the Department in April 1967. After two years of satisfactory performance, he was promoted in April 1969 to the position of area inspection supervisor. He was required to travel extensively, generally by car, to visit various food and drug manufacturing plants.

During the years 1971 and 1972, the Department learned that Mr. Cole occasionally failed to carry out certain inspections and the Department received some complaints about his indiscreet drinking. After investigation, the Department felt that the seriousness of these problems had been somewhat exaggerated and that the problems had been satisfactorily resolved. However, during the fiscal years 1970-1971 and 1971-1972, Mr. Cole was absent for various periods on sick leave for a total of 62 days. According to medical documents submitted by Mr. Cole, these absences were primarily due to a cervical disc problem, resulting from an old injury.

Then in September, 1973, while Mr. Cole was on a field trip to Penticton, British Columbia, it had been necessary for the Vancouver office to arrange for his transportation back to Vancouver after a Dr. Davidson in Penticton advised the office that Mr. Cole was in no condition to drive his car. His supervisors at the Vancouver office understood that Mr. Cole had re-injured his back. Following his return to Vancouver, he was under the care of Dr. A. D. Gray, who initially diagnosed the problem as "cervical disc protrusion." During the period from September 1973 to February 1974 he was examined also by Dr. T. H. Moore, an orthopedic surgeon, and by Dr. M. J. Roche, a psychiatrist. A report on Mr. Cole requested by the Department from Dr. Roche and dated February 9, 1974, read in part as follows:

> *Re: Mr. N. E. Cole*
>
> This forty-one year old employee of the Department of Health and Welfare was seen by me today at your request. His file and past history were reviewed from Mr. Davidson's file, which he had given me with all the pertinent findings relative to Mr. Cole's long history of problems with his neck dating back to 1963 and his more recent treatment having been in hospital in October 1973 for a short period with a diagnosis at that time of neck pain due to suspected cervical disc protrusion. He has since been seen by Dr. T. H. Moore in January, who feels that perhaps there was a functional overlay to this man's problem and certainly from his history I would feel that this is the case. I am not sure just what the state of his neck problem is, although Dr. Moore stated that he could find no evidence of a disc protrusion or root pressure.
>
> This man seems now to have gotten himself into a problem which has resulted in secondary anxiety related to financial matters and the fact that he has been off work and according to him has received no money for two months. He is applying for disability pension, but I note by Dr. Gray's last report that he could now resume work, but not to drive and apparently he has been offered a job in St. John's, at least temporarily. Certainly I feel that he would be capable of doing such work, although Mr. Cole has said at length that if he did this and "again got sick", he would "have nothing."

Mr. Cole had indeed applied for Disability Insurance on November 27, 1973 and although the Department had offered to employ him on light duties in the St. John's office early in 1974, Mr. Cole was reluctant to accept any employment while his claim for Disability Insurance was being processed. However, his claim was denied and he returned to work on April 21, 1974 after an absence of 98 days. In order to give him a chance to readjust and to prepare for returning to field work, Mr. Cole was given light duties in the St. John's office and he was not reassigned to his regular position until May 29, 1974. He was then given responsibility for a relatively small area, close to Vancouver, so that he could return home each evening. However, on Friday, June 8, at about 2:00 p.m., Mr. Connor, the Administrative Officer, received a call from Mr. Cole who was in New Westminster, British Columbia. Mr. Connor said later that Mr. Cole was hysterical and incoherent and that after he calmed down Mr. Cole, he learned that Mr. Cole had not completed his assigned inspections. Mr. Connor sent two other officers to bring Mr. Cole back to Vancouver where he was examined by Dr. Roche.

In a July 12, 1974 report to Mr. McCoy, the District Director, Mr. Connor stated that he had discussed Mr. Cole's case with Dr. Roche who informed him that Mr. Cole's depression was caused by feelings of guilt following heavy indulgence in alcohol and that he felt that alcohol was the root cause of Mr. Cole's problem. Mr. Connor also stated in his report that he had interviewed Mr. Cole on Monday, July 11 and Mr. Cole had admitted that he had been drinking heavily in New Westminster the week before. He had admitted also that he had been drinking frequently during his trips in June, July and August, just prior to his previous collapse in September, 1973.

On July 18, 1974, Mr. McCoy discussed with Mr. Cole his unsatisfactory performance and his drinking problem. Mr. McCoy told Mr. Cole that the Department recognized his problem as an illness and was willing to assist him to rehabilitate himself. However, he advised Mr. Cole to undertake a program of rehabilitation under the supervision of his physician. He warned Mr. Cole that his continued employment was jeopardized unless he took the necessary corrective action. The content of the discussion was confirmed in a letter dated July 18 and signed by both Mr. McCoy and Mr. Cole.

On July 25, 1974, Dr. Roche wrote to Mr. Connor as follows:

> I am replying to your letter of July 23, 1974 with regard to Mr. Cole whom I saw recently following an episode where he became very anxious and panicky while working in his position as an area inspection supervisor. There is no doubt that he did develop an acute anxiety reaction with marked phobic symptoms, fear of something happening to him which resulted in considerable agitation and restlessness. At that time he had to be brought back to Vancouver and I spent considerable time seeing both Mr. Cole and his wife.
>
> I feel at this time that on medical grounds Mr. Cole should not travel because of his rather acute anxiety, along with the fact that over the last year he had a number of other symptoms which are related to anxiety, which has been genuinely disabling to him.
>
> For this reason, I am recommending that for an indefinite period of time—at least until October or November—this man should not travel and at that time he should be reassessed as to any further recommendations.

Mr. Cole was again given light duties in the Vancouver area and was permitted to continue in this reduced capacity for more than three months. In the meantime, in a letter dated October 18, 1974, Dr. Roche wrote to Mr. Connor as follows:

> *Re: Mr. N. E. Cole*
>
> He shows little real anxiety today and many of the rather acute symptoms which he showed in the past are not noticeable at this time. He himself seems well-motivated to return to his regular position as area inspection supervisor and this was discussed with him at some length.
>
> On the basis of our interview today, it appears to me that Mr.

> Cole is now ready to resume his full time position as area inspection supervisor and is in my opinion now fit to travel without any specific restrictions.

Mr. Cole was assigned to his regular position and he made his first field trip on November 29, 1974. The Department again received adverse reports regarding Mr. Cole's conduct. Investigation by Departmental officers showed that during his field trips in the latter part of November 1974 and again during the week of February 14, 1975, Mr. Cole had indulged in excessive drinking. The Department decided to recall him from his regular work and to confine him to duties in the District Office.

On February 21, 1974, immediately after being recalled, Mr. Cole submitted the following letter to Mr. McCoy.

> I have come to the realization that my emotional problems will in the foreseeable future prevent me from assuming the responsibility of an inspection officer. I feel that I require an indefinite period of rehabilitation with the assistance of my physician and Alcoholics Anonymous and that part of this therapy would include my being near my family at all times. I realize that it is not fair to the Department or to my fellow workers to expect them to perform my duties as inspection officer for an indefinite period of time and for this reason, I respectfully request the Department to consider demoting me to a clerical position.
>
> If this request is granted, I promise to undergo such therapy and rehabilitative programs as may be necessary with the hope that some day in the not too distant future I could again assume the duties of inspection officer.

All this information was made available to the Deputy Minister of the Department who decided to recommend that Mr. Cole be released for incapacity under section 31(1) of the Public Service Employment Act. (See Appendix I.) Mr. Cole appealed against this recommendation and an appeal board was established by the Public Service Commission under section 31(3) of the Act to conduct an inquiry into the matter. (See Appendix I.)

Mr. T. G. Simon, who was Mr. Cole's representative before the Board, argued that the Department had failed to establish a case that justified its action to recommend the release of Mr. Cole. This action was too severe under the circumstances. Mr. Cole did not deny that he had a drinking problem, but his recent emotional problems and his breakdowns had been caused basically by his excessive work load and extreme fatigue. Prior to Mr. Cole's breakdown in September 1973, he had carried the heaviest work load of all inspection supervisors in British Columbia. Evidence of this was the fact that during Mr. Cole's absence following that breakdown, the Department had divided the area for which he had been responsible so as to reduce the work load. Moreover, Mr. Cole had been required to resume his regular duties without being given sufficient time to recover fully.

Mr. Simon contended further that Mr. Cole should have been appointed to another position where he could obtain medical assistance and be near his family. In February 1974, Mr. Cole had requested that he be demoted to a vacant clerical position. However, the Department failed to comply with his request and had appointed a person to the position who was much less qualified than Mr. Cole.

According to Mr. Simon, the events which had occurred while Mr. Cole was on field trips between September 1974 and February 1975, just before the Department's decision to release him, were disciplinary matters which did not properly fall under section 31 of the Act. These events involved allegations that Mr. Cole was drinking on the job and should have been dealt with differently. Mr. Cole should have received an initial warning. If he had failed to heed such a warning, he should have been suspended before any action was taken to release him. Moreover, if Mr. Cole had a drinking problem, there were procedures to be followed to insure that the appellant had had a chance to undergo a proper rehabilitation program before any action to release him was considered.

Mr. Simon also submitted in evidence two medical documents:

1. A letter from Dr. Roche, dated April 20, 1975, which read in part as follows:

> *Re: Mr. N. E. Cole*
>
> This man's mental status is such that in my opinion under relatively normal circumstances there appears to be no indication why he cannot carry on a full-time position. Whether this is the position which he has been working at would of course have to be decided by the Department in terms of their belief as to his capability of carrying on in that role.

2. A memorandum from Dr. R. J. Robinson, dated April 26, 1975, which read as follows:

> *Re: Mr. N. E. Cole*
>
> This gentleman has been under treatment for a low back syndrome history of herniated disc. He will be fit to resume full duties, including road travel, on May 8, 1975.

In conclusion, Mr. Simon stated that Mr. Cole was now capable of performing the duties of his position. Mr. Cole had joined Alcoholics Anonymous and he had not had a drink since February 21, 1975. He had now overcome his problem and based on the medical documents he had submitted, there was a responsibility on the Department to give him another chance.

In reply to the arguments presented by Mr. Simon on behalf of Mr. Cole, the Department's representative, Mr. P. A. Moyer, noted that Mr. Cole's physical and emotional problems did not originate with the events that took place during his field trips in November 1974 and February 1975. The problems had been building up over a period of four years and they had progressed to the point where he was not capable of providing satisfactory service and where his problems and actions could no longer be tolerated by the Department.

In regard to Mr. Cole's work load, the Department admitted that he had a heavy inspection schedule but it was not considered excessive and there was no evidence that this had been the cause of his problems. Moreover, Mr. Cole had never complained that his work load was excessive. It was the Department's policy to assign additional help when this was required in any area. During the periods of Mr. Cole's absence, his work was assigned to another employee who never complained of being overworked. Also, each time the appellant had been reassigned to his regular job after a period of illness and light duties, it was with the concurrence of both Mr. Cole and medical authorities. Mr. Cole's difficulties had no direct bearing on the changes made in the area boundaries in late 1973. These changes were made because of the establishment of an additional position for an inspection supervisor in British Columbia just at that time.

Mr. Moyer pointed out that when Mr. Cole returned from his September 1973 to April 1974 absence, he was assigned to a small area with reduced responsibility, which permitted him to return home nightly and to have much more frequent contact with the District Office in Vancouver. Yet Mr. Cole's problems reoccurred.

The Department had never considered Mr. Cole's case as one requiring disciplinary action. His absences had all been due to medical problems and his inability to control his drinking habits was considered to be an illness. The Department had attempted to assist him by counselling, by providing him with leave, and by employing him on light duties in the Vancouver area so that he could receive medical assistance and be near his home. The incidents of excessive drinking were only isolated events that were part of the total problem involved.

Mr. Moyer stated that he did not question the medical opinion contained in the two letters presented by Mr. Simon but noted that similar medical opinions had been given before. There was no assurance that Mr. Cole's problems would not appear again even if the Department gave him another chance.

Having heard this evidence, the members of the Appeal Board met to consider their decision.

Appendix I
Public Service Employment Act
Section 31

(1) Where an employee, in the opinion of the deputy head, is incompetent in performing the duties of the position he occupies or is incapable of performing those duties and should

(a) be appointed to a position at a lower maximum rate of pay, or

(b) be released,

the deputy head may recommend to the Commission that the employee be so appointed or released, as the case may be.

(2) The deputy head shall give notice in writing to an employee of a recommendation that the employee be appointed to a position at a lower maximum rate of pay or be released.

(3) Within such period after receiving the notice in writing mentioned in subsection (2) as the Commission prescribes, the employee may appeal against the recommendation of the deputy head to a board established by the Commission to conduct an inquiry at which the employee and the deputy head concerned, or their representatives, are given an opportunity of being heard, and upon being notified of the board's decision on the inquiry the Commission shall,

(a) notify the deputy head concerned that his recommendation will not be acted upon, or

(b) appoint the employee to a position at a lower maximum rate of pay, or release the employee,

accordingly as the decision of the board requires.

(4) If no appeal is made against a recommendation of the deputy head, the Commission may take such action with regard to the recommendation as it sees fit.

(5) The Commission may release an employee pursuant to a recommendation under this section and the employee thereupon ceases to be an employee.

12

Friends and Lovers

On June 13, 1973, a story headed "Lovers Reconciled in Court" appeared in an Ottawa newspaper. On June 27, Mrs. Jane Smith, one of the persons mentioned in the story, was informed by the Commissioner of the ABC Police that he had recommended her dismissal under section 31 of the Public Service Employment Act "due to circumstances surrounding her recent marriage." (See Appendix I.) Acting under section 31(3) of the Act, Mrs. Smith informed the Public Service Commission on June 29 of her intention to appeal against the Commissioner's recommendation. And on July 6, she sent another letter setting out the following grounds for her appeal:

1. Her recent marriage should have nothing to do with her employment in the public service.
2. The ABC Police, having failed in an earlier attempt to dismiss her, were now using sensational newspaper reports of a court case involving her husband as an excuse for dismissal action.
3. The dismissal notice contained general "nebulous" phrasing instead of clear reasons for the decision to take dismissal action.

On July 12, the Commission received a letter from the ABC Police stating that the recommendation for dismissal was based on Mrs. Smith's association with persons having police records, namely her husband and Mr. Terry Hogan who signed as a witness to her recent marriage.

The case for the ABC Police was presented to the Appeal Board by Mr. W. Turner, the Personnel Officer for the Police. He stated that the competence of Mrs. Smith and the performance of her duties were in no way factors in the decision to recommend her dismissal. The only reason for the recommendation was that, as a police organization, the ABC Police could not have on its staff anyone associating with known criminals. It was impossible, from an administrative point of view, to deny any member of the staff access to police files, records or current police information, much of which would be of value to criminals in the conduct of their illegal activities. Moreover, any member of the staff could "accidentally" destroy or mislay criminal records or other vital police information with little chance of detection. Members of the staff, therefore, must be as free as possible from any pressure exerted by the criminal element. A person married to a criminal was considered to be more than usually susceptible to pressure from this source.

Mr. Turner noted that in September 1972, Mrs. Smith, who was then Miss Jane Parsons, had crossed the United States border with three persons, two of whom had criminal records, namely Mr. Peter Smith and Mr. Terry Hogan. The United States federal authorities had reported the border crossing, as a matter of routine, to the ABC Police. In October 1972, on the basis of this information, the ABC Police had recommended the dismissal of Miss Parsons (Mrs. Smith). She appealed this recommendation and her appeal was upheld on the grounds that there had been no proof that she had been aware of the criminal records of her companions.

In January 1973, Mr. Smith had been charged with and convicted of theft. And in May 1973, Mr. Hogan had been charged with and convicted of breaking, entering and theft. In April 1973, Miss Parsons had married Mr. Smith and Mr. Hogan had signed as a witness to this civil marriage. Thus, Mrs. Smith could no longer claim ignorance of her associates' criminal records. She was, according to Mr. Turner, knowingly associating with active criminals and it was therefore essential to remove her immediately from the employ of the ABC Police.

Under the circumstances, the ABC Police had only two alternatives: to have Mrs. Smith transferred to another Department or to recommend her dismissal. She could not be laid off since a lay-off takes place only "where the services of an employee are no longer required because of lack of work or because of the discontinuance of a function." The ABC Police needed a clerk to replace Mrs. Smith at once.

Mr. Turner said that he personally had tried to arrange a transfer as early as January 1973 when he had written to the Public Service Commission requesting a transfer. When he had followed up this request several times by telephone, the Commission had informed him that the request was being processed in the normal manner. Then on June 26, the Commission informed Mr. Turner by letter that it had been unable to find a suitable position for Mrs. Smith.

Mrs. Smith was represented before the Appeal Board by Mr. George Green, an official of the Public Service Alliance of Canada. In response to questions from Mr. Green, Mr. Turner stated that Mrs. Smith had been employed as a clerk to the ABC Police for more than five years. She had entered the public service in 1968 at age 17 as a result of an open competition and after completing secondary school. Her efficiency rating forms showed she was a willing, competent and hard working employee and she had been promoted twice since 1968.

In reply to further questioning, Mr. Turner read aloud the criminal records of Mr. Smith and Mr. Hogan.

Mr. Peter Smith

1. May 1968—Auto theft—suspended sentence.

2. July 1968—Breaking Probation and Auto Theft—one year definite and one year indefinite.
3. September 1969—Attempted theft—fifteen days.
4. July 1970—Theft—four months.
5. January 1973—Theft—fourteen days.

Mr. Terry Hogan

1. February 1972—Shopbreaking—two months.
2. May 1973—Breaking, Entering and Theft—one year definite and one year indefinite.

Mr. Turner noted further that although people with criminal records may themselves be employed by the ABC Police, this practice has never applied to persons having "active" criminal records or to persons associating with "active" criminals.

On behalf of Mrs. Smith, Mr. Green stated to the Appeal Board that Mrs. Smith had simply married the man of her choice. She was aware of her husband's criminal record but her husband claimed that for three years he had not been, and was not now, engaged in criminal activities.

Mr. Smith's last conviction was the result of charges laid by Mrs. Smith "by mistake" before their marriage. Following a quarrel, Mr. Smith, to whom Mrs. Smith was engaged at the time, had driven to North Bay on a business trip. He took with him some of his fiancée's property which was in the trunk of his car. In a fit of pique, Mrs. Smith called the police and charged her fiancé with robbery. She had later tried to withdraw the charge, but the municipal police would not permit her to do so. She then appeared in court on behalf of her fiancé who was nevertheless convicted on technical grounds. He was sentenced only to the time he had spent in jail awaiting trial.

A local newspaper reporter who happened to be present at the court hearing had seized on the human interest aspect of the case and had reported the proceedings sensationally under the headline "Lovers Reconciled in Court." The newspaper report, Mr. Green contended, was both exaggerated and distorted. Thus, the charge and the conviction were the result of an unfortunate mistake by Mrs. Smith and could not in any way be considered evidence of criminal activity by Mr. Smith.

Moreover, Mrs. Smith was not actively associating with Mr. Hogan. Her only link with him was through her friend Miss Bernard who was a good friend of Mr. Hogan. In fact, the only reason Mr. Hogan had been present at her marriage was that Miss Bernard had agreed to be her bridesmaid. Since the time of her marriage, although Mrs. Smith and Miss Bernard lunched together frequently, Mrs. Smith had seen Mr. Hogan on only one or two occasions. It was difficult therefore to see how Mrs. Smith could be accused of associating with active criminals when her husband had been "going straight" for three years, and she had seen Mr. Hogan only once or twice in the past three months.

Mr. Green asserted also that the consequences of dismissal would be unnecessarily harsh. The dismissal would be noted on Mrs. Smith's permanent record, which would be available to future employers within the public service. Such a record would undoubtedly affect adversely her employment prospects. Further, the fact of dismissal would be made available on request to prospective employers outside government and would be a formidable obstacle to employment. In effect, dismissal would deprive Mrs. Smith of her means of livelihood. Mr. Green noted that the grounds for dismissal related only to the ABC Police. If Mrs. Smith had been assigned to a less sensitive department when she entered the public service, the question of dismissal would never have arisen.

Mrs. Smith testified that she was willing to accept a transfer and had in fact asked Mr. Turner to request a transfer immediately after her first appeal in late 1972. She said also that she was most anxious to transfer as soon as possible because of "the very awkward atmosphere in the office."

She stated that she had been interviewed by an officer of the Public Service Commission about the end of March 1973 but had had no other interviews. At the time of the Commission interview, she had asked whether a transfer had been arranged and had been told that the Commission "was working on it."

Mrs. Smith then informed the Appeal Board that her friend, Miss Bernard, had been transferred from the Department of External Affairs to the Department of Agriculture in October 1972. Miss Bernard had explained that a departmental personnel officer told her that she was being transferred "to a less sensitive department because of the type of people she was associating with." Mrs. Smith added that Miss Bernard had been the fourth person involved in the border crossing and that she assumed that the ABC Police had relayed this information to the Department of External Affairs.

Appendix I

Public Service Employment Act
Section 31

(1) Where an employee, in the opinion of the deputy head, is incompetent in performing the duties of the position he occupies or is incapable of performing those duties and should

(a) be appointed to a position at a lower maximum rate of pay, or
(b) be released,

the deputy head may recommend to the Commission that the employee be so appointed or released, as the case may be.

(2) The deputy head shall give notice in writing to an employee of a recommendation that the employee be appointed to a position at a lower maximum rate of pay or be released.

(3) Within such period after receiving the notice in writing mentioned in subsection (2) as the Commission prescribes, the employee may appeal against the recommendation of the deputy head to a board established by the Commission to conduct an inquiry at which the employee and the deputy head concerned, or their representatives, are given an opportunity of being heard, and upon being notified of the board's decision on the inquiry the Commission shall,

(a) notify the deputy head concerned that his recommendation will not be acted upon, or

(b) appoint the employee to a position at a lower maximum rate of pay, or release the employee,

accordingly as the decision of the board requires.

(4) If no appeal is made against a recommendation of the deputy head, the Commission may take such action with regard to the recommendation as it sees fit.

(5) The Commission may release an employee pursuant to a recommendation under this section and the employee thereupon ceases to be an employee.

13

Robbery or Delusion?

"I was robbed!" said Paul Reilly to one of his public service colleagues. "The Board was biased and unfair. I'm going to appeal its decision."

Mr. Reilly was referring to a competition for a position as a section head at the CO3 (Commercial Officer) level in the Department of Industry, Trade and Commerce. The Rating Board which assessed the candidates for the position found Mr. Reilly unqualified. The selection for the position was made by closed competition under the provisions of Section 7(1) of the Public Service Employment Regulations. (See Appendix I.) A closed competition is one in which only persons employed in the public service are eligible to apply. Twelve candidates for the position were assessed on the basis of appraisal reports contained in the Department's files and in the files of the Public Service Commission, the application form completed by each candidate, and individual interviews with the Rating Board.

The Board, composed of five senior departmental officials, assessed Mr. Reilly as follows:

> *Knowledge*
>
> This candidate has an M.A. in Economics. He served abroad as a Trade Commissioner in four different posts from 1960-1973. He states that he has been involved in Trade promotion and development in over forty different countries. As a direct result he has a good understanding of the problems involved in competing for markets abroad and of the competition to be expected from other countries. He has an academic bent and is very well informed in the sphere of market development.
>
> *Abilities to*
>
> a) *Analyze and Evaluate*
> The candidate seemed to be very mixed up in his evaluation of the recent Departmental reorganization and of the Department's objectives. He becomes over-involved in a project and does not seem to know when to let it go.
>
> b) *Plan*
> Although he has prepared a number of policy papers involving planning, very little direct implementation seems to have been effected as a result, indicating a lack in this attribute. His idea of complete flexibility to meet defined objectives is quite unrealistic.
>
> c) *Direct*
> He has not been able to accept direction from others, hence cannot expect to be too effective himself. He has had very little exposure to directing others during the past few years.

d) *Communicate*
Quite good demonstrated ability in this attribute. This is his strongest point, particularly in interpreting and research. He would enjoy lecturing in an academic atmosphere.

e) *Control*
Does not believe in conforming with approval goals without full flexibility of action. Does not understand the effect on other projects indicating a poor sense of priorities.

Potential for Effectiveness

Very inflexible and appears unable to adapt himself to changing conditions although he is a good thinker and innovator. A bit mixed up in his thinking and evaluation of Departmental objectives and unsure of the degree to which the Department should become involved vis-a-vis Industry. Does not accept the present bureaucratic set-up which he attempts to bypass, particularly if he realizes that his ideas are not going to be accepted one or two levels up. He is tactless and lacks a good deal of discretion with his superiors.

On the basis of failure ratings assigned to Mr. Reilly in regard to abilities to analyze and evaluate, to plan, to direct and to control and in regard to potential for effectiveness, the Board concluded that he was "not qualified" for the position.

Mr. Reilly appealed against the Board's decision under the provisions of Section 21 of the Public Service Employment Act. (See Appendix II.) At the appeals hearing, Mr. Reilly presented his own case; the Department was represented by Mr. J. McLeod, the Department's Chief of Staff Relations; and the Appeals Officer was Mr. K. Heron. In support of his appeal, Mr. Reilly (hereafter referred to as the appellant) contended that

1. The questions asked during the interview were not those appearing on the form prepared for this purpose and used in the assessment of other candidates.
2. The Rating Board based its decision to disqualify the appellant on a single appraisal report and on the interview, together with information appearing on the files. The Departmental file on the appellant was incomplete and no attempt was made to obtain a much more substantial confidential file on the appellant which is held in the Department. Moreover, despite the highly derogatory and apparently contradictory comments appearing in the single appraisal form, no attempt was made by the Rating Board to obtain the appellant's views on the Appraising Officer's comment that the appellant showed "poor judgement."
3. At no time during the interview was reference made to any initiative or activity on the part of the appellant which would reflect poor judgement. Since the Rating Board did not raise the issue of the adverse Appraisal Report, the appellant assumed that the appraisal would have

little bearing on the outcome of the competition and he was, therefore, misled.

4. The Appraisal Report does not describe adequately the appellant's performance.

5. The Appraisal Report is not an evaluation of professional competence, but has every appearance of an attempt to discredit an officer whose qualifications and productivity in trade promotion have drawn commendations from a wide variety of sources in government and in the business community. The overall impression of the Board's ratings is of a strong disposition not to qualify the appellant under any circumstances. For example, despite evidence in the application that the appellant may have few counterparts in the Department in his ability to "analyze and evaluate" and "plan," both of these categories were given failure ratings. Similarly, the ability to "direct" is rated a failure despite the contradiction such failure would constitute of the appellant's professional competence and success record.

Furthermore, the Board's assessment contains apparent contradictions. For example, the appellant is rated very highly in the "Knowledge" category but is said to be "very mixed up in his evaluation of . . . Departmental objectives." The appellant is an advocate of "complete flexibility" and "full flexibility of action" but is criticized under "Potential for Effectiveness" for being "very inflexible." He has on the one hand "good demonstrated ability" to communicate yet is on the other hand "tactless and lacks . . . discretion."

Also, the category of ability to "create and innovate" has been deleted even though these qualifications are clearly prerequisites to success in meeting competition from such sophisticated and more experienced sources as Japan, the United Kingdom, Europe and the United States. Since the appellant is well-known for these qualities, and there appears to be no other explanation for their exclusion, there is reason to suspect that an element of discrimination might have been present in their deletion.

6. The Rating Board failed to explore the circumstances leading to the accusation of poor judgement. Had it done so, it would have learned that the appellant was carrying out an assigned task on behalf of notable Canadian business interests and that he succeeded well in his assignment, identifying, because of his special knowledge and experience in the market, a number of economic opportunities offering unprecedented rewards to Canadian industry.

While the competence of individual members of the Rating Board is not in question, it is difficult to comprehend how an objective Board could reach the conclusion that a Departmental officer of almost unparallelled experience and success in trade promotion could be devoid of

"Potential for Effectiveness." It is even more perplexing to find that the appellant appeared to the Board "to be very mixed up in his evaluation of the recent Departmental reorganization and of the Department's objectives," subjects on which he has produced numerous incisive and lucid policy papers, examples of which were cited in his application.

On behalf of the Department, Mr. McLeod replied to the appellant's allegations as follows:

1. The appellant's qualifications were properly assessed by means of his application, an interview and an appraisal report. The appraisal form was accurate, having been concurred in by the Director of the Branch in which the appellant worked.

Questions were asked of all candidates in varying degrees of depth. If it was obvious that a candidate had a great deal of knowledge in a certain area, this area would not be pursued, because it was assumed that the candidate had a good knowlege of this area.

2. The chairman of the Rating Board requested the Personnel Office of the Department to submit the personal files of all the candidates. These files were used in the Board's assessment of all the candidates and they contained the relevant information required. The Rating Board took note of the appellant's objection to the appraisal, since the objection was written on the appraisal. It was the decision of the Department's personnel management not to supply his previous appraisal record which would presumably include his previous service as a Trade Commissioner.

3. During the interview, the appellant gave answers which reflected the fact that he uses poor judgement and is unwilling to follow instructions. This was confirmed in his appraisal. The issue of the appraisal was discussed at the time the appellant was appraised and the Rating Board did not find it necessary to discuss it with him further.

4. The Appraisal Report was prepared by his supervisor and agreed to by the Director of the Branch. It describes the appellant's performance adequately. The information prepared by the appellant was not acceptable to the Director or his supervisor, and was, therefore, not included in the performance appraisal. There is no requirement for management to make use of such material in any event.

It is notable that one member of the Rating Board was aware of the appellant's experience since he was his former supervisor. The decision not to qualify the appellant was, however, based on the interview and his most recent appraisal, not on the Board members' personal knowledge of his past performance. At the time that the appraisal was completed, it was not possible to foresee that a competition would be required to fill these positions and, therefore, there was no possibility of a conflict of interest at that time. The appraisal was completed on September 8, 1973 and the competition was announced on March 4, 1974.

The appellant had an opportunity, when he did not agree with the appraisal, to place this information on his appraisal in the form of an addendum but he did not do so. The Rating Board was, therefore, unable to use this information in the assessment of the candidate.

5. There is nothing unusual about letters of commendation concerning competence in trade promotion. The appellant's knowledge of export marketing is not in question since he met this requirement. The problem is that he applies his marketing competence in areas which at times are contrary to departmental instructions and policy. One of the requirements of the position for which he was considered is the use of good judgement.

The appellant has taken quotes from the Rating Board out of context. For example, an individual could advocate complete flexibility while at the same actually be very inflexible. The appellant has also compared comments relating to "Knowledge" with comments related to "Abilities" and to "Potential for Effectiveness."

Finally, the ability to "create and innovate" is not an essential qualification for a CO3 position and was therefore not rated by the Board.

6. The Rating Board came to the conclusion that the appellant lacked "Potential for Effectiveness" at this time for a position at the CO3 level based on his answers to questions asked at the interview and based on information in the Appraisal Report.

Mr. Heron, the Appeals Officer, then weighed the arguments presented by the appellant and by the Department as a basis for deciding whether the appeal should be allowed or dismissed.

Appendix I

Public Service Employment Regulations
Section 7(1)

Every appointment shall be in accordance with selection standards and shall be made

a) by open or closed competition; or

b) by other process of personnel selection

(i) from among employees in respect of whom data is recorded in an inventory which employees meet the qualifications for the appointment, or

(ii) where no employee referred to in subparagraph (i) is qualified and suitable for the appointment, from among applicants who are not employed in the Public Service in respect of whom data is recorded in an inventory, which persons meet the qualifications for the appointment.

Appendix II
Public Service Employment Act
Section 21

Where a person is appointed or is about to be appointed under this Act and the selection of the person for appointment was made from within the Public Service

a) by closed competition, every unsuccessful candidate, or

b) without competition, every person whose opportunity for advancement, in the opinion of the Commission, has been prejudicially affected,

may within such period as the Commission prescribes, appeal against the appointment to a board established by the Commission to conduct an inquiry at which the person appealing and the deputy head concerned, or their representatives, are given an opportunity of being heard, and upon being notified of the board's decision on the inquiry the Commission shall,

c) if the appointment has been made, confirm or revoke the appointment, or

d) if the appointment has not been made, make or not make the appointment,

accordingly as the decision of the board requires.

14

The Auditor's Lament

Mr. James Weston had been employed for six years as an auditor in the Moose Jaw office of the Department of National Revenue (Customs and Excise). It was his responsibility to audit the books of firms liable to pay sales tax. His immediate supervisor was Mr. Robert Hunter. The District Manager at Moose Jaw was Mr. William Thomas and the Regional Director of Excise Tax Administration, stationed at Regina, was Mr. David Anders.

Normally, auditors like Mr. Weston work out of a district office but spend most of their time in the offices of the firms whose books they are required to audit. The auditors, who use their own automobiles to travel between the district office and these firms, are compensated for the automobile expenses they incur.

An itinerary is kept in the district office so that supervisors will know where an auditor is working and where he can be reached. It is important that the office be kept informed of each auditor's movements. The Department must rely on an auditor's loyalty and sense of responsibility to be at work for at least the required seven and one-half hours per day. Regular hours are supposed to be from 8:40 a.m. to 4:40 p.m. with one-half hour off for lunch. Since most of the general audit work is performed at a licensee's place of business, supervision must often be by "remote control."

On December 13, Mr. Weston received a letter dated December 11 from Mr. Thomas which formally advised him of the loss of one day's pay and warned him that "besides the loss of one day's pay you shall on any further occurrences of misconduct be severely reprimanded." The letter was headed "Disciplinary Action on Absence from Assigned Duty on December 2."

Mr. Watson presented a grievance against his loss of pay on the grounds that a financial penalty had been imposed on him for disciplinary reasons and that the penalty was not justified under the circumstances. (See Appendix I for the relevant sections of the Public Service Staff Relations Act.) As Mr. Watson proceeded through the various stages of the grievance procedure, he received the following responses to his grievance. Mr. Nason wrote on January 6 that

> The loss of one day's pay (December 2) from your salary occurred because we felt that you did not work on this day. This decision was reached after careful consideration of all the pertinent facts of your case, and for the following two reasons:

> 1. You did not report to your assigned work location.
> 2. You did not report to your supervisor when you found that your automobile required repairs.
>
> Therefore, your grievance is denied.

The Regional Director, Mr. J. N. Leigh, wrote on January 20 as follows:

> Upon reviewing all the facts in your case, I concur with the 1st step answer, that your loss of pay occurred because you did not work the day of December 2 from 9:30 a.m. to the end of the day. However, one hour's pay will be returned to you because of your attendance at the office until 9:30 a.m. of December 2.

Then, Mr. Donald Hope, Director of Personnel Administration, wrote on February 19 that

> Your loss of pay has occurred as a result of your not having worked on December 2 from 9:30 a.m. to the end of the day. It is considered that you had full opportunity to account for your actions during this period.

Mr. Weston's grievance was then heard on April 16 by an adjudicator of the Public Service Staff Relations Board. The adjudicator heard the following evidence.

Mr. Weston testified that on November 20 of the previous year, he had received a memorandum from Mr. Hunter instructing him to complete an audit at the firm of V. B. Greening. The memorandum read in part as follows:

> You are to employ yourself there, during the ensuing business days, in your capacity as an Excise Tax Auditor II, to finalize the audit now in progress.
>
> You are relieved of the necessity to report at the Moose Jaw District Excise Tax Office, complete other assignments presently in progress, or submit forms E155 until the Greening assignment is completed.

Mr. Weston said that he continued the Greening audit until Tuesday, December 1. Since the work required extensive use of a calculating machine, he went to the district office on the morning of Wednesday, December 2 to make use of the office calculator. He stated that he had the permission of Mr. Thomas, the District Manager, to do this and Mr. Thomas later confirmed this statement. However, at some time between 9:30 a.m. and 10:00 a.m., Mr. Weston was instructed by his supervisor, Mr. Hunter, to leave the office machine and return to the Greening firm. In the absence of Mr. Thomas for the day, Mr. Hunter was senior supervisor. Mr. Hunter had advised Mr. Greening that Mr. Weston would be returning, but later in the afternoon, he was told by Mr. Greening that Mr. Weston had not arrived.

On Thursday, December 3, Mr. Weston worked at the Greening office from 9:00 a.m. to 5:30 p.m. He continued working there on Friday morning until the lunch hour, when he kept a dental appointment at 1:00 p.m. and then went to his own office. That afternoon, he reported on his work to Mr. Hunter and was eventually asked where he had been on Wednesday.

Mr. Weston claimed that Mr. Hunter refused to listen to any explanation and took him to see Mr. Thomas who said he would have to give up a day's pay because he had not been at work.

On Tuesday, December 8, Mr. Weston met again with Mr. Hunter and Mr. Thomas. Mr. Weston testified that he was rebuked for his absence on Wednesday and was reminded that one day's pay would be deducted from his salary. He said also that his attempt to relate what had happened received no serious consideration and that he was not even allowed to complete his explanation.

Mr. Weston then testified that while he was at the office on the morning of Wednesday, December 2, he had been given a telephone message from a Mr. Finch at Stewart Bros. Ltd. who wished some advice regarding sales tax. The delivery of this message was confirmed by the office secretary, Miss Sandra Corbett. She testified that she frequently got calls from business men needing information and advice and that she placed the messages on auditors' desks. Mr. John Parsons, one of the other auditors, testified that he sometimes received such inquiries and that if necessary he went to see the taxpayer without seeking or receiving specific authority from his supervisor. Mr. Weston said that he had known Mr. Finch for many years and that he had decided to see him briefly on the way to the Greening firm which was in the same area. He said also that he had spent the better part of an hour with Mr. Finch because the problem was more complex than he had anticipated.

Mr. Thomas contended that Mr. Weston had no authority to audit an unlicensed business interested in obtaining refunds. In his letter of December 11 to Mr. Weston, Mr. Thomas had written:

> Since you were advised by written memo on November 20, by your supervisor, to pursue the audit of V. B. Greening Ltd. and not attend at any other employment until this audit was completed, you took upon yourself the responsibility of going to Stewart Bros. Ltd., who by the way are not licensed.

Moreover, Mr. Hunter testified that during a private conversation on December 4, Mr. Weston "indicated" that after leaving the office he had not gone to the Stewart firm but to his home because he believed that it was too late in the morning to go to the Greening office before lunch.

Mr. Weston did not give evidence in reply to refute Mr. Hunter's version of the affair, but his sworn testimony was that he had spent time with Mr. Finch discussing a sales tax problem.

Mr. Weston testified that he had intended to proceed to the Greening office immediately after lunch. However, he had to visit a service station to correct a malfunction in the engine of his car. When he was leaving the station, the rear window suddenly shattered "into a thousand pieces", presumably due to extreme cold. Mr. Weston then called his insurance agent, Mr. Jake O'Neill, who referred him to the firm of K. Bunting Ltd. which agreed to replace the rear window. Mr. Weston said that the job took from about 2:30 p.m. to about 4:00 p.m. He said also that the broken window created a serious hazard in winter conditions with no visibility to the rear, and that it would have been imprudent for him to proceed by car to the Greening office immediately after lunch.

Mr. Weston also said that it was common practice, when necessary, for auditors to take time during working hours to have urgent repair work done on their cars. Indeed, on one occasion, he himself had been instructed by Mr. Thomas to drive Mr. Thomas' car to the garage for repairs, which took about one-half of his time on duty. This incident was confirmed by Mr. Thomas.

Mr. Weston was home by 4:00 p.m. or about forty minutes before his normal quitting time. He testified that it was too late to return to the Greening office, that he had decided to work at home, and that he did so for three and one-half hours. He said that he often worked in off-duty hours at home. Moreover, he thought that it would have been negligent to leave the car at the Bunting garage, because the car contained confidential and official documents as well as the Greening audit papers.

Mr. Thomas testified that auditors are forbidden to perform their work at home and that this had repeatedly been made clear to Mr. Weston and to other auditors. Mr. Hunter testified that he considered a reprimand to be more serious than the deduction of a day's salary. He said: "I do not feel disciplinary action was called for. I warned him there would be reprimands for any further offences. We did not impose a penalty on him; we just didn't pay for a day he didn't work."

Appendix I
Public Service Staff Relations Act
GRIEVANCES

Right to Present Grievances

90. (1) Where any employee feels himself to be aggrieved

(a) by the interpretation or application in respect of him of

(i) a provision of a statute, or of a regulation, by-law, direction or other instrument made or issued by the employer, dealing with terms and conditions of employment, or

(ii) a provision of a collective agreement or an arbitral award; or

(b) as a result of any occurrence or matter affecting his terms and conditions of employment, other than a provision described in subparagraph *(a)*(i) or (ii),

in respect of which no administrative procedure for redress is provided in or under an Act of Parliament, he is entitled, subject to subsection (2), to present the grievance at each of the levels, up to and including the final level, in the grievance process provided for by this Act. . . .

Adjudication of Grievances

Reference to Adjudication

91. (1) Where an employee has presented a grievance up to and including the final level in the grievance process with respect to

(a) the interpretation or application in respect of him of a provision of a collective agreement or an arbitral award, or

(b) disciplinary action resulting in discharge, suspension or a financial penalty,

and his grievance has not been dealt with to his satisfaction, he may refer the grievance to adjudication.

15

Mr. Smith's Expense Accounts

Mr. Ralph Smith worked in four different field offices of a large government department between 1970 and 1975. As he moved from one city to another during that period, he rose rapidly in rank from a PE2 (Personnel Administrator) to a PE6. His work was described by his superiors as outstanding. In 1975, he was 41 years of age and was fluently bilingual.

Mr. Smith had served in the Canadian Army from 1952 until his resignation from the Army in 1962. He was married in 1955 and has one child. The marriage broke up in the summer of 1975 and his wife now resides in another province from that in which he works. He attributes the failure of his marriage in part to the fact that his wife resented frequent moves while he was in the Army and later in the public service.

Each of Mr. Smith's moves between 1970 and 1975 were connected with promotions and each move involved considerable expense, all of which was paid for by the government under the Removal Expense Regulations established by the Treasury Board.

After Mr. Smith's last move in 1975, the Director General of the Region which Mr. Smith had just left sent a confidential memorandum to Mr. T. R. Clark, the Assistant Deputy Minister (Operations) of the department. The memorandum, dated May 19, 1975, drew attention to certain irregularities in Mr. Smith's expense accounts, all connected with his move from one city to another in the summer of 1974. Mr. Clark consulted Mr. A. C. Gow, Assistant Deputy Minister (Administration), and an investigation was undertaken by Mr. D. R. Peters, Chief Expenditure Accounting, at the departmental headquarters.

Mr. Peters reviewed the expense account referred to headquarters by the Regional Director and reported in mid-June that "there has definitely been a conscious effort to defraud the department of at least $88.76 and robably much more. . . . There was a definite pattern of erasures and alterations to receipts." He also reported that a *preliminary* review of all of Mr. Smith's accounts from 1970 to 1975 (about 80 in all) suggested that there were "many entries further verification would confirm as being fraudulent."

One June 13, Mr. Clark met with Mr. Smith in Winnipeg and informed him of the serious nature of the situation and of the ongoing investigation. Mr. Clark confirmed this in writing on June 16.

In his final report to Mr. Gow on July 28, Mr. Peters stated:

> I have found no discrepancies in the petty cash accounts, imprest accounts or training allowances paid by Receiver General cheques during Smith's tenure of office. There were, however, several anomalies in his travel and removal expense claims. . . .

He then described three "spurious receipts," several receipts not in agreement with hotel records, several apparent duplications of charges claimed and paid, certain claims alleged to exceed the allowances provided by the regulations and certain questionable taxi charges. He estimated the "overcharges" at $292.06 extending from July, 1970 to March 1975.

On August 4, Mr. Gow sent the Peters report to Mr. Clark with a number of comments, including the following:

> Serious anomalies were discovered in the claims submitted. However, no discrepancies were found in other areas of financial responsibilities involving this officer . . . .
>
> The balance of the report concerns itself with anomalies and discrepancies, particularly with receipts that have been altered or fail to coincide with hotel records. In some instances, investigation indicates that there is no hotel at the place for which the expenses are claimed as supported by the receipt in question. . . .
>
> My personal opinion is that the audit and review does not disclose any criminal act. However, you may wish to seek the advice of the Department Legal Adviser in this respect. It is my opinion that the efforts to manipulate receipts by changing dates, etc., were a deliberate attempt to deceive in a manner which is unacceptable, particularly by a person holding a position of responsibility in this Department. . . .

Mr. Clark wrote to Mr. Smith on September 3:

> The Department has now completed a thorough review of your expense accounts and has uncovered a number of significant irregularities which . . . will require the Department to take action. Before doing so, however, we wish to provide you an opportunity to respond to the evidence, if you so desire.

Mr. Clark included with this letter a copy of Mr. Peters' observations and the documents on which these were based.

Mr. Smith replied on September 11. The most pertinent sections of his letter are as follows:

> Thank you for the opportunity to respond to the evidence presented to you. I regret that through my ineptitude in handling my personal affairs I have given you and the Department reason to question my integrity as well as the time and concern involved in the investigation and interviews.
>
> Unfortunately until recently I have not paid sufficient attention to my personal circumstances but have left financial and other details to my wife. The results have been less than satisfactory. Following our move in 1974, a list of expenses together with supporting receipts and documents were delivered to my secretary for the claim submission. The list was retained on file and is enclosed. When the submission was questioned by Regional Office I responded in what

must have seemed a brazen manner since I assumed that all was in order. Had I attempted to defraud, I suppose my reaction to their frequent telephone inquiries and letter from the Director of Operations would have been to accept the reduced amount proposed.

Until your discussion with me I had no idea that the truthfulness of the claim was in question but rather assumed that interpretation of regulations was the issue. On reading the report I can understand and appreciate your position on this matter. I cannot transfer responsibility since I signed the claim but I hope you will consider the circumstances.

Where receipts for travel or accommodation in the North do not agree with records, I cannot recall the instances nor can I explain why I claimed less than the hotel records indicate I paid. Where taxi or water transport was involved, I frequently carried supplies or equipment with me or if accompanied by a Departmental employee, I paid for both of us rather than have claims submitted for such small amounts.

Travel in the North is seldom a matter of personal taste and charges for it vary with circumstances. On one occasion I managed to hitchhike (by air) to remote reserves with Indian Affairs. The condition was that I contribute for food and accommodation at usual allowance rates. In that instance you would find that I claimed for meals but no transport. On more than one occasion when ticketed to fly Ford Airways, I was obliged to return to the office by rail or wait for weather which would have resulted in longer stays in the North. You might be interested in determining how much of my travel was done on weekends or at night.

My interest and enthusiasm for the Department are in no way diminished by this incident and I will continue to implement its policies to the best of my ability. I have never been dishonest in dealings with my superiors nor knowingly have I attempted to falsify personal claims or any other document.

As suggested in the report, recovery action is indicated and I have no objection to this being done. I realize that my explanation in no way excuses my haphazard approach to my personal affairs but hope that you will take into account my performance in the administration and management of departmental business.

Mr. Clark considered that the reply did not address itself to the specific evidence presented. He informed Mr. Smith on September 27 that he had concluded that it was his duty to recommend "disciplinary action" to the Deputy Minister. He discussed alternative forms of disciplinary action with the Deputy Minister, including suspension, demotion and discharge. Mr. Clark recommended discharge.

On November 24, the Deputy Minister sent an official notice of discharge to Mr. Smith. The first two paragraphs of his letter read as follows:

On September 27, 1975, Mr. T. R. Clark, Assistant Deputy Minister (Operations), informed you that he had no option but to recommend strong disciplinary action, in respect of your failure to provid

> him with an acceptable explanation of certain financial irregularities uncovered in a review of your expense accounts.
>
> As a result of his recommendations and my review of the facts, I have decided regretfully that your employment with this department must be terminated. Therefore, under the authority delegated to me, pursuant to Section 106 of the Public Service Terms and Conditions of Employment Regulations, I am hereby discharging you from the Public Service, effective upon the close of business October 31, 1975.

Mr. Smith appealed against this decision and evidence was heard by an adjudicator of the Public Service Staff Relations Board.

Since some of the items questioned by Mr. Peters in the 1970-1973 period were open to a number of different interpretations, the government decided to rely on six items relating to the period July 2, 1974 to August 17, 1974 when Mr. Smith and his family were moved from one city and one Region to another. These items were as follows:

	Hotel	*Amount*	*Action*
July 2, 1974	Dominion	$18.00	Altered as to date and amount.
July 8, 1974	Hillcrest	56.00	Hand written receipt substituted for hotel bill.
July 10, 1974	Dominion	36.00	Motel records show 32.50 paid for July 8-10. Full amount already deleted as being in excess of 5 days.*
August 3, 1974	Riverview	19.00	No such hotel in city.
August 16, 1974	Dominion	18.00	Not located in city claimed.
August 17, 1974	Hillcrest	38.50	Alterations to dates of arrival and departure.

Mr. Smith himself signed all the accounts in question, certifying that they were correct. The actual words of the certification are:

> I hereby certify that I have expended the amounts indicated, that the account is correct and just in all respects, and that the whole expenditure was actually incurred on government business.

On the basis of this evidence, counsel for the government argued that Mr. Smith's discharge resulted from a "very obvious attempt" by Mr. Smith "or by someone for whom he was responsible" to defraud the Crown. He emphasized the distinction between a claim made (when in

---

*Section 14A of the Removal Expense Regulations allowed a maximum of 5 days of expenses for a "Househunting Trip".

doubt) over and above the amounts authorized, which may be made in good faith, and on the other hand the submission of forged vouchers with intent to deceive.

Counsel contended also that even after being confronted by Mr. Clark and even after receiving Mr. Peters' report, Mr. Smith had several months in which to offer an explanation, a period during which he knew the matter to be very serious. The explanations he gave were minimal and unsatisfactory.

Counsel argued further that even if fraud was not proved, Mr. Smith had been guilty of gross negligence which was all the more serious by reason of the employee's high level of responsibility and experience. It was a grave matter for any employee to certify a false account and entirely inexcusable for an employee of Mr. Smith's rank and intelligence.

Counsel for Mr. Smith admitted that by signing the accounts, Mr. Smith had been guilty of negligence but he claimed that the penalty of discharge was excessive when the offence was that of negligence and not fraud. He emphasized also that when Mr. Smith had worked in other field offices, he had access to accounts which are maintained to permit the speedy issue of emergency assistance cheques to persons in need. These accounts had all been audited and all were in order. There is no evidence that Mr. Smith ever knowingly obtained public money improperly or dishonestly.

Moreover, the fictitious vouchers and the altered vouchers were the work of a very stupid person—and nobody can suggest that Mr. Smith is a very stupid man. The "forgeries" were so obvious that they could have been detected by any alert junior clerk who took the trouble to look at them. There is insufficient evidence to permit the inference that they were done deliberately in such a way as to get Mr. Smith in trouble, but such an explanation is not beyond the bounds of possibility.

Counsel for Mr. Smith noted that the total amount involved in the six items discussed is $185.50. Of that total, $36.00 was certain to be disallowed in any case becaue the regulations did not permit payment of meals and lodging beyond five days on a "Househunting Trip." This leaves a balance of $149.50 which would have been the net gain if the "forgeries" had gone forever undetected. It represents a very small proportion of the cost to the public treasury of moving the Smith family from one city to another.

It is not probable that a man of Mr. Smith's intelligence, on reading his accounts and the attached vouchers, would fail to recognize that they contain both errors and deceptions which invite detection, and therefore invite a penalty. When a man sets out to commit fraud, he does not often advertise his intentions so brazenly. Moreover, the changes made manually in several receipts and two receipts which appear to be fictitious do not appear to be the work of a masculine hand.

Mr. Smith then testified that he was preoccupied with his duties after arriving at his new job, and he therefore left the preparation of all expense accounts to his wife and also to his secretary, suggesting that they consult Mr. S. C. Gardner, Chief of accounting services in the regional headquarters. He asserted that he had very little knowledge of the matter from that point on, except that there were numerous communications back and forth between his wife and Mr. Gardner. He also had the understanding that his wife and his secretary, not being familiar with the Expense Removal Regulations, would claim as much as possible and be guided by Mr. Gardner as to reductions or disallowances which would have to be made under the regulations. He testified firmly that he did not scrutinize the so-called receipts or vouchers attached to the accounts or the details set out in the accounts themselves. What he did do was to sign all the accounts in the space provided and certify them to be correct, relying on the documentation collected by his wife and relying also on Mr. Gardner to disallow whatever might not be allowable. He did not deny that there have been alterations or forgeries in the receipts mentioned above, but insisted he was not aware of them when his accounts were submitted.

Mr. Smith testified also that during the period in question, his marital relationship was deteriorating. However, he continued to rely on his wife with respect to financial matters to the point where his wife could sign cheques drawn on any of his several bank accounts. He also entrusted expense accounts to his wife in the belief that she would negotiate their validity with Mr. Gardner.

He stated further that his inadequate explanations to Mr. Clark in 1975 were attributable, at least in part, to the collapse of his marriage. Immediately after Mr. Clark confronted Mr. Smith with evidence of fraud, he telephoned his wife and asked for an explanation. At the time of this incident, the marriage was breaking up and indeed was on its way to court. According to Mr. Smith, his wife's reply to his request for an explanation was "that's your problem." She refused to co-operate in defending her husband.

16

Reality or Appearance?

"Progressive Marine Limited" was incorporated as a private company under the Business Corporations Act on September 14. Its head office was shown as 224 Fairfield Avenue, Etobicoke. The directors of the company were listed as John William Hogan, Vincent Richard Smith, Joseph Andrew Thompson and Daniel James White.

The address of the head office was also the address of Captain John William Hogan, a supervisor of nautical services in the Marine Safety Branch of the Ministry of Transport which was based at Toronto. The position was one of considerable responsibility and required high qualifications and long experience in marine services. Captain Hogan supervised several other employees and could authorize overtime as well as the taking off of time in lieu of collecting overtime pay. The other three directors were employees in the Ministry of Transport working under Captain Hogan's supervision.

On November 2, Captain Hogan signed a letter as President of Progressive Marine Limited which was sent to a number of firms in the marine industry on the Great Lakes. In the letter (reproduced in Appendix I), Captain Hogan offered a variety of services and commodities to these firms. The letterhead read "Progressive Marine Limited" and in smaller type: "Marine Sales and Services." The address given was the same as Captain Hogan's residence.

On November 12, Captain Thomas Hammond, Regional Superintendent at Toronto, reported to Captain Robert Cole, the Regional Director of Marine Services for the Central Region, that he had received a complaint from a member of the shipping community regarding the letter sent out by Progressive Marine. During a visit to Montreal earlier in November, Captain Cole had heard a more informal complaint from an official of the Shipping Federation. He had discussed the complaint with Captain Gerald March, the Chief of Nautical Services at Ottawa.

When Captain Cole investigated the whole matter, he learned that Smith, Thompson and White were associated with Captain Hogan in Progressive Marine Limited. He learned also that during the past summer Mr. Smith had adjusted the compasses on two Canadian Coast Guard vessels and had charged a total of $145. for these services. The accounts were at first rejected by the District Finance Officer of the Ministry of Transport because they were in Smith's name and he was known to be an employee of the Ministry. Smith then resubmitted the invoices to the District Financial Officer in the name of "Prime Marine Consulting Ltd., 224 Fairfield Avenue, Etobicoke." There was no such company as "Prime Marine Consulting Ltd." but Captain Hogan and Mr. Smith apparently had that name in mind before they obtained incorporation under the name of Progressive Marine.

As a result of his inquiries, Captain Cole arranged a meeting in his office with Captain March and Captain Hogan on December 28. The discussion centred on Item 6 of Captain Hogan's letter whereby Progressive had offered "marine superintendence of the loading or discharge of specialized and liquid cargoes." In view of Captain Hogan's regulatory, licensing and other responsibilities, it was suggested to him that such services could come into conflict with his official duties. Captain Hogan responded that he "would be willing to delete number 6."

Captain Cole pointed out to Captain Hogan at the meeting of December 28 and at another meeting on December 29 that there were other services offered by Progressive Marine which could be embarrassing to the Ministry. He also gave Captain Hogan a copy of Order-in-Council P.C. 3/1440 of March 21, 1951 which provides *inter alia* that no full-time employee of the government shall engage in any gainful employment or occupation outside of his regular duties which is of such a character as would bring the public service into disrepute or in which the employee "would exploit undesirably the acquaintance with his fellow employees or with others which arises directly out of his employment in the public service", or in which the employee "will make use of restricted, confidential, or secret information acquired by him as a result of his employment . . . ." It is also provided by P.C. 3/1440 that the deputy head may direct an employee to terminate or limit his outside employment when in the opinion of the deputy head it prevents the employee from carrying out his duties or impairs his efficiency. Captain Hogan insisted at both meetings that there was no conflict of interest and that he had done nothing to which legitimate objection could be taken.

On January 7, Captain Cole forwarded his report to Mr. J. McLeod, the Deputy Administrator of the Ministry's Marine Services and recommended that the Deputy Minister consider the desirability of requiring Captain Hogan to cease his outside activities.

Then, on January 9, Captain Hogan submitted a report to Captain Cole in which he explained the current services offered by Progressive and stated that

> The services offered were selected and are performed so that there can be no real or apparent contravention of the requirements of PC3/1440.
>
> The performing of those services requiring technical expertise, e.g. compass adjusting, when done by company members takes place on their own time, in most instances. On the rare occasion a service is requested to be performed during normal working hours the time taken is in lieu of overtime. The carrying out of these services does not, nor will it be permitted to, interfere with the performance of Departmental duties. It is difficult to state the number of

> hours involved as the services are provided in response to orders and are thus irregular. Experience to date indicates approximately three (3) hours per week. Any service hours required, in excess of those available to the technical staff, would be supplied on a contractual basis by other qualified persons resident in this area.
>
> The business is conducted during regular office hours by staff unconnected with the Public Service from an office located in Etobicoke, Ontario.

Captain Cole sent the report to Deputy Administrator McLeod with the suggestion that it be "looked at". The problem remained under review at Ottawa for more than three months and then on April 30 Captain Cole was informed by his superiors that the Deputy Minister required the four Progressive directors to choose by May 10 between their work with Progressive and their work with the Ministry of Transport. The four directors were informed of this decision at once.

By May 10, Smith, Thompson and White gave written assurance to Captain Cole that they had ceased to perform duties for Progressive. Captain Hogan, however, presented a grievance on May 14 under section 90(1) of the Public Service Staff Relations Act. (See Appendix II.) He complained against the ultimatum he had received on May 10 and he requested the following corrective action:

> That I be provided, in detail, item by item, with the information which led to and the reason for the request, in order to refute the charges which have apparently been brought against me.

The grievance was promptly referred to headquarters and resulted in a meeting at Ottawa on May 20 at which Mr. R. Davis, Administrator of the Canadian Marine Transportation Administration, received Deputy Administrator McLeod, Captain Cole and Captain Hogan. The problem of conflict of interest, whether actual or potential, was discussed and hypothetical examples were put to Captain Hogan, who remained adamant in his view that he was not involved in a conflict of interest. On May 22, Mr. Davis informed Captain Hogan by letter that he must choose between his association with Progressive and his employment with the Ministry of Transport and that he should make his choice known by May 30. On May 27, Captain Hogan wrote Mr. Davis asking that his grievance go to a higher level, although he had already been assured that the Deputy Minister demanded a clear answer from Captain Hogan as to his choice between Progressive and the Ministry, and had decided that no employee could be permitted to work for both at the same time. In his reply of June 5, Mr. Davis suspended Captain Hogan. The concluding paragraph of his letter read as follows:

> Having regard to the fact that you have not given notice of your intentions I have no alternative but to advise you that you are sus-

> pended without pay from the performance of your duties with the Ministry of Transport until further notice. This suspension will take effect from such time as this letter is given to you.

On June 18, Captain Hogan presented the following grievance under section 91(1) of the Public Service Staff Relations Act. (See Appendix II.)

> I grieve that I was improperly suspended on June 5.

He requested the following corrective action:

> Full compensation for time lost. I further ask for a declaration that I am entitled to work during non-working hours for Progressive Marine Limited.

The grievance was referred to the final level without delay and a reply was given on July 2 by Mr. H. Johnson, Senior Assistant to the Deputy Minister of Transport in the Deputy Minister's absence. The reply read in part as follows:

> Your involvement with Progressive Marine Limited has now been the subject of at least three meetings between yourself and senior Ministry managers. During these meetings, it was explained to you that the Ministry regards your association with Progressive Marine Limited as being in serious potential conflict with your responsibilities as a Nautical Services Officer. Examples of situations where conflicts could reasonably arise or appear to exist were discussed with you. You also had an opportunity to present your views on this matter.
>
> Having regard to the fact that you had not given notice of your intentions, and apparently continued your association with Progressive while remaining an employee of the Ministry, you were suspended by Mr. Davis effective June 5 and until further notice. The Deputy Minister concurs entirely with this action.
>
> The Deputy Minister is satisfied that you understand his position in this matter and what is required of you, and that you have been provided with ample information in this regard. Nonetheless, to avoid any possibility of misunderstanding, I am hereby repeating his direction to you to terminate your association with Progressive Marine Limited if you wish to continue your employment in the Ministry.
>
> As a Nautical Services Officer, you have extensive regulatory enforcement, licensing, adjudication and other responsibilities which can and do have a significant financial and other impact on individuals and organizations in the marine industry. In exercising such responsibility, you are in large part acting on behalf of the Ministry under the Canada Shipping Act. You must not only *be* fair and objective, you must *appear* to be fair and objective. If you engage in private business activities, regardless of the precise nature of those activities or the hours during which they are conducted, with some

of the same individuals or organizations with whom you have, or are likely to have, official Ministry business, the Ministry's impartiality in discharging its responsibilities is put in doubt. This the Deputy Minister is not prepared to allow.

I want to emphasize again that your personal integrity, honesty or responsibility is not in question, nor is there any intention to infringe on your individual rights and freedom. On the other hand, I hope you appreciate that a conflict of interest may arise even where the employee is innocent of any wrongful intent or design, and that if you continue your association with Progressive, you could become involved in a conflict situation without advance notice and under circumstances that you cannot avoid. Even the appearance of a conflict of interest may impair your effectiveness as a public servant, in addition to embarrassing the Ministry and bringing the Public Service of Canada into disrepute.

In his letter to you of June 5, Mr. Davis outlined the alternatives open to you. You are hereby required to communicate your decision in writing to him no later than July 11. If you fail to make your intentions known by this date, or if you continue your association with Progressive Marine Limited while remaining an employee of this Ministry, the Deputy Minister shall have no alternative but to consider further disciplinary measures, up to and including discharge.

The suspension of Captain Hogan continued in effect from June 5 until August 12. On August 12, he was notified by Captain Cole that he could return to work on the following day; he did in fact return on August 12. The recall was the direct result of a letter addressed to Mr. Johnson, written by Captain Hogan on August 8 and apparently received in Captain Cole's office at noon on August 9, and in Mr. Johnson's Ottawa office in the afternoon of August 10. It read in part as follows:

Dear Mr. Johnson:

I wish to inform you that I have ceased to perform any services for Progressive Marine Limited save and except for the early completion of the documents, etc., required of me to completely divest myself of all association with that corporation, a condition of my reinstatement in my position with the Ministry of Transport.

Captain Hogan handed over certain activities of the company to his wife. For example, on August 19, one week after his reinstatement, he wrote a letter (under the letterhead of Progressive) to one of Progressive's customers which read as follows:

I refer to the Agreement, Authorized Nautical Chart Agent, signed by me in July on behalf of Progressive Marine Limited.

That company is undergoing a voluntary wind-up at the request of some of its Directors and I have found it necessary to open a new Company to supply the same services to our existing customers, as well as retain a source of supply for new customers.

> Would you therefore, as indicated by Section 7 of the Agreement, accept this as a change of name of Company from Progressive Marine Limited to Advance Marine and forward for completion a new Agreement. The new owner is my wife, Jane Hogan, and there is no change in address or telephone number.

In early November, Captain Hogan's grievance of June 18 was heard by an adjudicator of the Public Service Staff Relations Act. During the hearings, Captain Hogan testified in regard to his August 19 letter to a customer that

> They (the customer) sent a new agreement to Jane, who now sells charts. That's her business now. Her last position was Purchasing Agent for a manufacturing firm in Etobicoke. She was the office clerk for Progressive . . . . Her business is with yachtsmen.

Captain Hogan also testified that the new firm, named "Advance Marine," was owned by his wife Jane and that the purpose of the new firm was "to succeed Progressive," but on a limited scale.

Among the arguments presented by Mr. Anderson, counsel for Captain Hogan, was the contention that there was no evidence of an actual conflict of interest and that Captain Hogan had a reputation for integrity. With reference to the Order-in-Council (P.C. 3/1440) relating to outside employment, Mr. Anderson said that it is not clear as to what kinds of activities "would bring the public service into disrepute" or which "would exploit undesirably the acquaintance with his fellow employees or with others which arises out of his employment in the public service." He argued also that the Order-in-Council referred to "a factual situation" when it authorized the deputy head to take disciplinary action with respect to outside employment which prevents "the employee from carrying out his duties in the public service or impairs his efficiency."

Appendix I

Dear Sir:

Progressive Marine Limited is pleased to announce to you the formation of this new supplier of marine goods and services.

Employing a technical staff, all of whom hold the highest grade of Masters Certificate issued by Canada, we offer our services in the shipping fields listed:

1. Compass adjusting, fleet prices available;
2. Trials master for new construction. Services 1 and 2 will be combined upon request;
3. Ship delivery;
4. Ship movement;
5. Marine Consultant;

6. Marine Superintendence of the loading or discharge of specialized and liquid cargoes;
7. Surveys:
   (a) On hire/off hire;
   (b) Deadweight;
   (c) Sale/Purchase.

Additional to the services outlined we are accredited sales agents for nautical charts and publications of the:

1. Canadian Hydrographic Services, Marine Sciences Branch, Department of the Environment;
2. United States Lakes Surveys, U.S. Department of Commerce;
3. United States Ocean Surveys, U.S. Department of Commerce.

As you are aware, the recently implemented Charts and Publications Regulations have placed a greater emphasis on the carriage of up-to-date editions than was heretofore the case. In this regard, we would be pleased to have a representative discuss your requirements with you and arrange to have your chart and publication requirements kept current by automatic supply of new editions. This would relieve you and your Masters of the necessity to place individual orders and ensure that each of your vessels is supplied simultaneously.

We would also be pleased to discuss supplying you with compass adjustment on a regular basis so that the compass certificates and deviation cards required to be carried by each vessel would always be current.

Nautical text books and associated publications and small marine instruments are sold. It has been our observation and experience that the seamen of Central Canada have been hard pressed in the past to obtain these items. We offer a centralized location from which those of your staff studying for certificates or just interested in keeping up-to-date can purchase the latest editions. If your Company has a central technical lending library available to its officers, we would be pleased to include its up-dating with the previously explained chart service.

Although a new Company, we feel we can offer you unsurpassed technical advice and assistance, as well as the finest service, on the waters of Central Canada.

Appendix II
Public Service Staff Relations Act
Section 90(1)

90. (1) Where any employee feels himself to be aggrieved
   (a) by the interpretation or application in respect of him of
      (i) a provision of a statute, or of a regulation, by-law, direction or other instrument made or issued by the em-

ployer, dealing with terms and conditions of employment, or

(ii) a provision of a collective agreement or an arbitral award; or

(b) as a result of any occurrence or matter affecting his terms and conditions of employment, other than a provision described in subparagraph (a)(i) or (ii),

in respect of which no administrative procedure for redress is provided in or under an Act of Parliament, he is entitled, subject to subsection (2), to present the grievance at each of the levels, up to and including the final level, in the grievance process provided for by this Act.

Section 91(1)

91. (1) Where an employee has presented a grievance up to and including the final level in the grievance process with respect to

(a) the interpretation or application in respect of him of a provision of a collective agreement or an arbitral award, or

(b) disciplinary action resulting in discharge, suspension or a financial penalty,

and his grievance has not been dealt with to his satisfaction, he may refer the grievance to adjudication.

17

Public Interest or Collective Interest?

In 1974, a number of employees working for a federal department in a large Canadian city outside Ottawa began to complain about their work load. These employees worked under a collective agreement between the government as their employer and a national public service staff association, and all were members of a constituent of the staff association, namely the Canadian Association of Social Security Employees (CASSE).

The complaints led to the holding of a meeting on June 7, 1974, called by Mr. Michael Roberts, Director of District No. 9 of CASSE. The geographical boundaries of the District were the same as those of the city.

The 90 persons who attended this first meeting appointed a committee of 6 persons to study the problems involved, to try to find solutions, and to prepare a report with recommendations, principally with regard to the work load of the employees. The people present at this meeting also decided that this report should come before a formal meeting, properly constituted, on June 23, 1974, of the delegates for the District. All members of the Union in the District were invited to this meeting and all had a right to speak but only delegates elected by the locals had the right to vote. On June 23, about 180 persons attended of whom 24 were delegates duly elected by the various locals in accordance with the by-laws of CASSE. (CASSE had about 600 members in the District of whom about half were employees who were directly interested in this problem.)

The decision taken at the meeting was to file a collective grievance and to go before the mass media five working days later via a press conference in order to present the problems involved to the public itself. A draft press release was submitted at the meeting but was not accepted by the delegates. It was decided to give a mandate to the committee to make further revisions and corrections before going before the mass media at a press conference.

The press conference was held at the Superior Motor Inn on June 28. At the head table at the press conference were Mr. William Kerr and Mrs. Joan Miller. Mr. Kerr was President of one of the locals of the Union in the District. Mrs. Miller opened the press conference and Mr. Kerr fielded most of the questions.

In her opening statement, Mrs. Miller stated that the purpose of the conference was not to denigrate the principles and programs put forward by the Department, which were on the whole rather avant-garde, but to prove that the human and material resources necessary to give proper attention to the needs of the public and to apply the Department's programs efficiently were not available. The opening statement contained some criticism of government policies and programs and was not just a criticism of working conditions. Moreover, the actual press release prepared by Mr. Kerr and Mrs. Miller went much further. The financial policies of the government, in so far as its subsidization of the Department's programs is concerned, were attacked. Quotes from the Economic Council of Canada, from the leader of an Opposition political party and from a former government Cabinet minister who was now critical of the government's social security programs were used to support the argument that the Department spent more money per capita in other provinces. The press release contained other criticisms and concluded with a series of recommendations relating to the objectives and methods used in the programs of the Department as well as to the working conditions.

Mr. Kerr admitted at the press conference that he and his colleagues had deliberately chosen the period of the federal election campaign to make public their complaints because during an election campaign such publicity would be more effective. On the same day as the press conference, Mr. Kerr was interviewed on television in regard to the employees' grievances. Several newspaper articles on the subject appeared on the following day.

On the day of the press conference, the acting regional director for the Department was Mr. David Walden, who was normally director of operations. He was temporarily replacing the regional director who was out of the city on government business. Mr. Walden had been aware of a certain malaise among the personnel in the Department, in as much as some of the employees had been complaining about their work load and there had been articles in the newspapers during the week before the press conference discussing such complaints and the possibility of a press conference. When the proposed press conference came to Mr. Walden's attention, he wanted to stop it because he felt it was unauthorized and illegal. He did not, however, want to prohibit the press conference with a direct order which might have been perceived as an attempt to influence or intimidate the Union and therefore as a violation of the Public Service Staff Relations Act (see appendix A). He did, however, try to stop the press conference by advising union officials in the district not to hold it. He also sent two representatives to monitor the press conference and he himself monitored the televised interview.

Then, on July 2, Mr. Walden established an investigatory committee composed of senior departmental officials working in the city. The committee began deliberations on July 5 and reported on July 10. On July 5,

Mr. Walden suspended Mr. Kerr and Mrs. Miller pending an inquiry into the whole matter.

During its investigation, the Committee learned from Mr. Michael Roberts, director of the District for CASSE, that the delegates at the June 23 meeting and the members of the ad hoc committee considered themselves legally authorized to act as they did. The Committee learned from discussions with the suspended employees that they had acted as a group and not as individuals and that they believed that they were duly and legally authorized to hold the press conference. Mr. John Corbett, the regional President of CASSE, whose jurisdiction included District No. 9, informed the Committee that he had never authorized the press conference. Moreover, when he heard that the press conference was going to take place, he telephoned Mr. Roberts and advised him not to attend the press conference. He also telephoned Mr. Kerr and advised him not to hold the press conference. Mr. Kevin Shane, the business agent for CASSE in the region, told the Committee that he had on several occasions attempted to dissuade the members of the District from holding a press conference. He felt that the District Council had only a recommending or consultative function and could not take such a decision without referring the matter to the regional executive. At the meeting of June 23, he told the delegates that any decision taken there would be without value and could even lead to placing the District in trusteeship or to the expulsion of persons from the Union.

The Committee felt that the by-laws of CASSE were somewhat ambiguous on the powers of the districts and it could not determine whether a district could take such action as a press conference with relation to working conditions. The only reference to the powers of the district in the by-laws is in article 15(a) which provides that the district functions as an administrative organ on behalf of the regional council, and deals with subjects of a particular interest for the local sections within the district. It is notable that on July 7, the National President of CASSE sent a telegram to the Minister and the Deputy Minister of the Department informing them that the principal spokesman at the press conference was the president of a local (Mr. Kerr) and that he spoke not merely as an employee but as an officer of the Union.

The Committee also felt that the defamatory criticism of the Department, which, in its opinion, had taken place, would not have been legitimate in any event, whether the Union had authorized it or not, as it would not have been a legitimate Union activity.

In its report, the Committee recommended a disciplinary sanction for Mr. Kerr and Mrs. Miller which could be as serious as discharge.

On November 15, Mr. Kerr and Mrs. Miller were suspended for two months beginning on July 6 and ending on September 5. The two employees filed grievances against both their original July 5 suspension and against the two months' suspension imposed on them.

The grievances were submitted to adjudication under the Public Service Staff Relations Act. Counsel for the employer argued that those who participated in the press conference were not legally authorized by CASSE to do so and their acts must therefore be considered as those of individuals and not of representatives of the Union duly authorized to speak on its behalf. Nothing in the by-laws of CASSE permits a district to hold a press conference. Moreover, the press conference had been opposed by the regional president, John Corbett, and by the regional business agent, Kevin Shane.

Counsel for the employer contended also that employees may not criticize the policies, programs nad services of their Department or of the government in public, even if the Union may have the right to criticize working conditions under the terms of sections 6 and 8 of the Public Service Staff Relations Act. (See Appendix I.)

Furthermore, the Information Manual of the Department contains guidelines for employees with regard to communications with the public. Clause 4.06 of this guide provides specifically that departmental officers and their staffs must not indulge publicly in criticism or adverse comment on established governmental or departmental policy, programs, services, etc. This article also prohibits officers and their staffs from engaging in public controversy and debate on policy matters and contains other similar directives. According to Mr. Walden, this guide, along with other guides covering other subjects, was readily available in all departmental offices and its contents should have been known by the employees concerned.

Counsel for the employer also asserted that Mr. Walden could not have prohibited the press conference and was afraid of producing counter-productive effects by any action he might take other than that actually taken by him which did attempt to dissuade those involved from holding the press conference. It was impossible for Mr. Walden to know in advance to what extent the press conference would be criticizing the programs and services of the Department. Mr. Walden acted in good faith in imposing temporary suspensions pending the inquiry, as the infractions seemed serious. The Public Service Staff Relations Act does not permit press conferences to be held as a legitimate union activity even for the purpose of criticizing working conditions, although it is admitted that these may take place from time to time.

Counsel for the grievors argued that the press conference had been held within the framework of a union activity resulting from an express mandate received at the district level on June 23. The local members and the local district director believed that this was a legal union activity and the grievors acted in the name of the Union and as spokesmen for the Union members. The legality of the mandate, according to the grievors, as a legitimate union activity, derives from article 15(a), of the CASSE by-laws. The district is situated mid-way between the local sections and the region and the activity in question is permitted by these by-laws. The grievors believed that Mr. Corbett, the regional president of CASSE, had no authority or right of veto over a decision to hold a press conference.

The grievors also argued that the employer's action in disciplining them constituted an intervention in legitimate union activities in violation of sections 6 and 8(2) of the Public Service Staff Relations Act. If the employer had any legitimate complaint, it should have exercised its resources against the entire membership of the Union and not merely against the persons who were delegated by the local Union with the responsibility of holding the press conference.

Moreover, the information guide was not accessible to the grievors. They never saw the guide before the press conference was held. They only received the extract from it on July 2, several days after the press conference.

Furthermore, it was argued that the grievors were all acting in good faith with a view to obtaining better service for the public and for the employees of the Department. The content of the press conference was honest and not virulent. A real problem existed, as is recognized by the representatives of the employer, and the existence of the problem was already known to the public through various newspaper articles prior to the press conference in question.

Appendix I

Public Service Staff Relations Act

Sectons 6 and 8

6. Every employee may be a member of an employee organization and may participate in the lawful activities of the employee organization of which he is a member.

8. (1) No person who is employed in a managerial or confidential capacity, whether or not he is acting on behalf of the employer, shall participate in or interfere with the formation or administration of an employee organization.

(2) No person shall

(a) refuse to employ or to continue to employ any person, or otherwise discriminate against any person in regard to employment or any term or condition of employment because the person is a member of an employee organization or was or is exercising any right under this Act;

(b) impose any condition on an appointment or in a contract of employment or propose the imposition of any condition on an appointment or in a contract of employment that seeks to restrain

an employee or a person seeking employment from becoming a member of an employee organization or exercising any right under this Act; or

(c) seek by intimidation, by threat of dismissal or by any other kind of threat, or by the imposition of a pecuniary or any other penalty or by any other means to compel an employee

(i) to become, refrain from becoming or cease to be, or

(ii) except as otherwise provided in a collective agreement, to continue to be,

a member of an employee organization, or to refrain from exercising any other right under this Act;

but no person shall be deemed to have contravened this subsection by reason of any act or thing done or omitted in relation to a person employed, or proposed to be employed, in a managerial or confidential capacity.

18

The Kroeker Case

In 1952, Mr. John Kroeker, an actuary, joined the Department of Insurance (a branch of the federal Department of Finance).

By the spring of 1964, it appeared that the government intended to adopt a Canada pension plan. Although Mr. Kroeker's superiors had been aware of his reservations about the proposed plan for almost a year, they continued to seek his actuarial advice on it. The Superintendent of Insurance agreed with Mr. Kroeker's suggestion that the senior officers of the Department should meet to discuss the implications of the plan since the Department had done a considerable amount of work on it.

This meeting was not held and Mr. Kroeker felt that his superiors did not want an objective discussion of the plan. Then, on April 14, 1964, in a statement to the Canadian Association of Actuaries, he urged the Association, as a professional group, to make representations to the government on the plan. He also pointed out the flaws he found in the plan.

On the following day, the Superintendent of Insurance informed Mr. Kroeker that his action had not been "in the best British tradition". The Superintendent said that he did not want Mr. Kroeker's resignation, but that he wanted to be told in advance if Mr. Kroeker again "contemplated doing this type of thing".

Between May and August 1964, Mr. Kroeker utilized other avenues to oppose the plan. He sought personal and confidental interviews with members of Parliament and business leaders. He also sent letters to the Prime Minister and to all provincial Premiers recommending changes in the proposed plan. He took these actions as a private citizen and apparently without his superiors' knowledge.

In September 1964, Mr. Kroeker's superiors asked him to compare a white paper on the Canadian Pension Plan prepared by the Department of National Health and Welfare with the bill drafted for the consideration of the House of Commons. Although he indicated his reluctance to give advice on a bill to which he was opposed, he gave his professional advice as an actuary upon instructions from both the Superintendent and the Chief Actuary.

On March 1, 1965, while he was on leave, Mr. Kroeker called a conference in the Press Gallery of the House of Commons and read a severe indictment of the Canada Pension Plan, then under consideration in the House. Excerpts from his lengthy statement include the following:

> There is no reasonable basis on which this plan can become law. At best, it is well-intentioned bungling. At worst, it is a colossal fraud on all Canadians . . . . The plan is not the child of reason and liberty. It is a creature of propaganda and fear. . . .
>
> As to the nature of the plan, it is first and foremost unwarranted Big Government forcing its way into the life insurance field. Public enterprise moves in on private enterprise for no established reason. Its entry is on an artificially flavoured basis because of its compulsory nature and because of its regulatory powers over established private insurers. If private enterprise has failed in this area, we should be told how. If there is no protest, what is to prevent Big Government from starting to print newspapers, build houses, make cars, etc., etc., at the times and under the conditions of its choice? Civil service or ministerial empire-building is not easily stopped. . . .
>
> Support for the plan is more apparent that real. Few Canadians have given it serious thought. Fewer still feel they understand it. Even so we were told by a Cabinet Minister a year ago: "This is something that everybody wants, and I can't believe that anyone will knock it on the head." In my opinion, this plan certainly deserves a "knock on the head", and, if it were widely understood, it would be withdrawn quickly and permanently from Parliament's consideration. . . . Many Members of Parliament are afraid they don't understand the plan, afraid of its actuarial label and afraid to vote against it for fear their voters won't understand.

On March 4, the Superintendent of Insurance notified Mr. Kroeker that he had decided to recommend his dismissal on the following major grounds:

1. Mr. Kroeker "should not have made a public statement of his personal views attacking an important matter of Government policy."
2. The Government cannot have confidence in an employee who has launched a public attack on its decisions, particularly when the employee occupies a senior position.
3. On a number of occasions during the past year, Mr. Kroeker "was told by his superiors not to make public statements of his personal views critical of matters of Government policy, since such action would be incompatible with his position as a civil servant."

In his notice of appeal, dated March 17, Mr. Kroeker contended:

1. There is no law prohibiting a person employed in the Civil Service from making a public statement of his personal views attacking, criticizing or commenting favourably on matters of Government policy.
2. The reason given by the Superintendent of Insurance for his decision to recommend dismissal is contrary to the Canadian Bill of Rights.
3. The reason given by the Superintendent of Insurance is inconsistent with the reason given in the official report of the House of Commons Debates dated March 1, 1965:

> Mr. Gene Rheaume (Northwest Territories): In view of the information given to the House earlier today that Mr. Kroeker had been dismissed for making public certain views he held, would the hon. lady assure the House that those federal officials who testified before the special parliamentary committee on the Canada Pension Plan were not operating under the same sort of threat?
>
> Hon. Judy V. LaMarsh (Minister of National Health and Welfare): I disagree with what the hon. member has said. There was no suggestion from my colleague the Minister of Finance that this man was being relieved of his responsibilities because of what he said. It was because, being a civil servant, in the course of his position he said something which was contemptuous of parliament.

During his testimony before the three-man appeal board appointed by the Civil Service Commission, Mr. Kroeker argued further that he had never received written advice not to express his views on government policy while employed as a civil servant. He did admit, however, that two successive Superintendents of Insurance had informed him that "it was not the thing to do." Mr. Kroeker noted that some time between April and September 1964 the Chief Personnel Officer of his Department told him that there were no written regulations on the subject and that he should "let common sense prevail." Mr. Kroeker admitted also that his superiors had never directed him to do anything "which would put him in professional disrepute."

Mr. Kroeker asserted, however, that he had cause for his belief that the government would permit civil servants to comment on government policy. In 1965, a top official in the Department of National Health and Welfare had expressed with impunity his personal views of the Canada Pension Plan in an article for the *Financial Post* entitled "Your Guide to Pensions in Canada." Moreover, two weeks after Mr. Kroeker's dismissal, an official of the Department of the Secretary of State was quoted in the *Ottawa Citizen* as saying that as a matter of principle none of the government's suggestion awards should be taxed.

Finally, Mr. Kroeker stated that he had taken an oath of office and secrecy promising that he would not reveal any confidential information obtained through his civil service position. He noted, however, that the facts in his public statement were public knowledge and that the opinions expressed were his own.

19

A Sensitive Position

The Canadian Radio-Telecommunications Commission (CRTC), formerly the Board of Broadcast Governors, was established in 1968. The CRTC is a regulatory agency which reports to Parliament through the Minister of Communications. It is authorized to regulate and supervise all aspects of the Canadian broadcasting system, namely radio, television and cable television. The powers of the Commission are described in the Broadcasting Act and include the authority to prescribe classes of broadcasting licences, to establish regulations applicable to all licence holders relating to various specified matters (such as program standards, allocation of broadcasting time which may be devoted to advertising and partisan political broadcasting, the operation of broadcast networks, and other related matters) and to revoke licences, except those issued to the Canadian Broadcasting Corporation.

As a result of a heavy workload during 1971 and early 1972, the CRTC decided to hire an additional legal counsel. Treasury Board authorized a classification for the position of assistant Counsel for the CRTC at a salary level between $14,685. and $21,602. On February 7, 1972, the Public Service Commission appointed Miss Cindy Eaton to this position. Among the duties assigned to Miss Eaton were these:

> a) Provides the Radio-Television Commission with legal advice on new and existing regulations and policies:
>
> (i) By assessing whether broadcasters would adhere to proposed regulations.
>
> b) Interprets legislation relating to the regulation and supervision of the broadcasting industry in order to counsel commissioners and staff on the jurisdiction of the commission:
>
> (i) By giving opinions on such laws as the Elections Act in Canada, the Bank Act and laws applying to copyright and free speech;
>
> (ii) By giving opinions on the legal basis for allegations that infractions have been committed and by advising whether the Commission should prosecute or take other action.
>
> c) Represents the Commission on interdepartmental committees to ensure that the objectives are reflected in new legislation and in government policies:
>
> (i) By questioning representatives of interest groups making presentations on future legislation, and government policy:
>
> d) Acts as the Commission's counsel at public hearings:
>
> (i) By studying applications for licences and interventions, staff comments and relevant commission policy and previous decisions;
>
> (ii) By framing and posing questions to elicit further facts and comments from applicant and interveners to aid the commissioners in making a decision on the application;

(iii) By advising the Commission that evidence being given by parties to an application is inconsistent with the application or intervention submitted to ensure that each party has had the opportunity to examine the other's presentation before the hearing.
e) Conducts litigation on behalf of the Commission when provincial jurisdiction permits the lawyer to practise, conducts prosecutions of licensees of broadcasting undertakings, and prepares memoranda of fact and law for appeals to the Supreme Court of Canada and the Federal Court of Canada.
f) The work also requires representation of the Commission in cases before the Supreme Court of Canada and the Federal Court of Canada. When provincial jurisdiction permits, the work also involves conducting prosecutions of licensees of broadcasting stations who are believed not to comply with the Broadcasting Act and Regulations. Such prosecutions could involve fines of as much as $25,000 to $50,000.

When Miss Eaton reported to work on February 7, she mentioned to her director, the General Counsel of the CRTC, that she was deliberating as to whether she would seek the nomination to run as a Liberal candidate in the constituency of Ottawa Centre. The General Counsel expressed concern about Miss Eaton's possible absence from work because of the heavy workload of the Commission. She said that it was not likely that she would seek the nomination.

On February 24, the General Counsel raised the matter again with Miss Eaton and repeated his concern about her possible absence. Once again, she said that she was not likely to seek the nomination.

Then, on March 3, Miss Eaton informed the General Counsel that she intended to seek the nomination and to announce her candidacy on March 6. She was given a copy of section 32 of the Public Service Employment Act (reproduced in part in Appendix I) as well as advice on the procedures she should follow. She was specifically advised that section 32 seemed to require that a public servant receive a leave of absence from the Public Service Commission before announcing publicly an intention to seek nomination.

On March 6, Miss Eaton presented to the CRTC a letter she had addressed to the Public Service Commission requesting a leave of absence. On March 7, Miss Eaton's attention was again drawn to the requirements of section 32. Then, on March 8 and 9, an announcement of her intention to seek the nomination appeared together with her picture in the Ottawa newspapers. And on March 9, the CRTC's Director of Personnel, in the presence of the General Counsel, informed Miss Eaton that she had contravened the Public Service Employment Act.

Also on March 9, Mr. Pierre Juneau, the Chairman of the CRTC, was informed that the practices of the Public Service Commission required him to write a letter to the Chairman of the Commission giving his opinion as to whether the usefulness of the employee in the position she then occupied would be impaired by her candidacy. Mr. Juneau wrote the following letter, dated March 9:

> Mr. J.M. Carson
> Chairman
> Public Service Commission
> Place de Ville, Tower "A"
> Ottawa, Ontario
>
> Dear Mr. Carson:
>
> Miss Cindy Eaton, a lawyer employed in the Legal Branch of the Canadian Radio-Television Commission since February 7, 1972 has informed me that she has applied to you for the necessary leave of absence without pay to seek nomination as a candidate and, if successful, to be a candidate for election as a member of the House of Commons.
>
> Considering the duties being performed by Miss Eaton, in a regulatory agency of a quasi-judicial nature, it is my view that should she be successful or decide to withdraw and return to her present position, her usefulness would be considerably impaired by reason of having been a candidate for election as a member of the House of Commons. As a lawyer in the CRTC, Miss Eaton would be expected to have contact with officials and lawyers of business and other establishments who deal with the Commission in an adversary relationship.

The Public Service Commission immediately studied Miss Eaton's request for leave of absence and decided to deny the leave of absence on the grounds that Miss Eaton's usefulness as assistant Counsel would be impaired by her candidacy. The Secretary of the Commission informed Miss Eaton of this decision in writing on March 10.

The Director of Personnel and the General Counsel then met with Miss Eaton. She was informed that under section 32 of the Act, the CRTC would be obliged to take disciplinary action if she did not take steps to comply with the Act. In a letter to Miss Eaton on March 13, the Director of Personnel asked her what course of action she intended to take. She answered in a letter to the Chairman of the Public Service Commission that she would continue to seek the nomination. Mr. Juneau, Chairman of the CRTC, then gave Miss Eaton a letter suspending her on the grounds that she had contravened the Public Service Employment Act. March 13 was her last day of work.

The whole matter was raised in the House of Commons with the result that on March 15 "the subject matter of the refusal of the Public Service Commission to grant leave to Miss Cindy Eaton, a lawyer with the CRTC, to seek a political nomination" was referred to the Standing Committee on Broadcasting, Films and Assistance to the Arts.

Portions of the evidence presented to this committee on March 20 and March 21 are reproduced below:

Mr. McCleave: My understanding of the term "candidate for election" would be somebody who had been nominated to run in an election, not somebody who was seeking to be nominated to run in an election. I wonder, therefore, how it is that this problem has possibly arisen. One would think that Miss Eaton, or anybody else for that matter, would be quite outside the operations of this act until such moment as there was a candidate for whom Miss Eaton worked. I presume it is broad enough to cover herself, if she were in fact a candidate, but I do not think it is broad enough to cover her if she was merely expressing an intention to seek to be a candidate.
Mr. Juneau: Mr. McCleave, I think this is a matter of policy, and I may stand to be contradicted on this but we do not consider that it is the responsibility of the CRTC to interpret the Public Service Employment Act. We were told by the Public Service Commission that Miss Eaton was not being granted leave of absence and we acted on that. We made no decision of any kind before we received that official opinion of the Public Service Commission.

Mr. Stewart: I am interested in this from several points of view, Mr. Juneau. As you may or may not know I was a public servant and I sought nomination as a public servant with a leave of absence. Perhaps my duties had not been considered particularly sensitive but I feel that the experience I have had as a public servant has enhanced my usefulness as a member. I dare say that if I return to the public service one day my experience as a member will also enhance my usefulness in the public service. I find the statement of the duties difficult to understand: in this letter to Miss Eaton it said that "your duties are such that your usefulness to the public service would be impaired." I cannot understand how the services of a person who wants to serve the people as a member of Parliament and therefore wishes to seek nomination would thereby be impaired. I dare say there is any number of public servants who have very partisan feelings, who do not dare express them and whose usefulness would be considerably impaired according to this way of thinking. I fail to see the fact this person has expressed the desire publicly to seek nomination would put her in a position where her judgement would be impaired or where her dealings in future would be impaired. It is the judgement of the Public Service Commission that I question and it is the judgement of the CRTC in supporting the decision of the Public Service Commission that I question.

Mr. Rose: I presume that you were the ultimate decision maker in her appointment, where you? You decided whether or not Miss Eaton was to be hired?
Mr. Juneau: No. The Public Service Commission does that.
Mr. Rose: She was hired by the Public Service Commission, then, but were you aware that Miss Eaton had worked on behalf of candidates for the Liberal Party previous to her appointment in her particularly sensitive position?

Mr. Juneau: I am sure you will be surprised but I did not. I did not know Miss Eaton; I did not know her name before it was mentioned to me that she was a candidate for that position in the CRTC.
Mr. Rose: Yes, I am surprised. I am shocked even, as I think it is pretty well-known that Miss Eaton had been very active on behalf of certain Liberal candidates in the past.
Mr. Juneau: As you know my activities are not altogether in that field.
Mr. Rose: Were her immediate superiors aware of her previous political interests?
Mr. Juneau: I do not think they were. I have checked that very carefully and there is no reference whatsoever in Miss Eaton's application to her so-called political interests. I have her application here and there are all kinds of questions asked there. Some of them have to do with her professional qualifications and membership in all kinds of societies. There is not one reference by her to membership in any political party.
Mr. Rose: Did Miss Eaton sit for a competition for this particular position?
Mr. Juneau: I think you had better ask the Public Service Commission. She was appointed according to the usual procedures of the Public Service Commission, whether you would call that a competition, I do not know.
Mr. Rose: It depends on the level; the usual procedures depend upon who it is. Some people sit for competitions and others do not.

I was wondering, sir, if you could tell me, since you said in your letter that her effectiveness might be impaired by the fact that she had assumed a more partisan role than that of simply a solicitor or a lawyer for the public service, if this was on the grounds of a political interest or was it because the CRTC could little afford to give her time off to campaign? What was the basic reason?
Mr. Juneau: The basic reason was the second one. There is no question that when you badly need a lawyer or, for that purpose, any other employee at that level—this was a very important level—and we very badly needed another senior lawyer, and you learn the day after you have hired that person that she probably is going to go on to do something else, it does not help your operations. However, that was not the reason.
Mr. Rose: It was not?
Mr. Juneau: No, it was not.
Mr. Rose: It wasn't the time off?
Mr. Juneau: No, the time off was not the reason.
Mr. Rose: I see.
Mr. Juneau: It was an inconvenience, but presumably it is one we would have had to put up with.
Mr. Rose: It was the fact that her decision-making powers in her relationships with her colleagues and other people with whom she might rub shoulders in her official capacity might be impaired or biased because of her partisan views, is that so?
Mr. Juneau: Yes, I think I could put it this way. I think if the wording of the act is to be taken seriously, presumably there are cases where usefulness will be impaired, so we have to start from the basis that

there are cases where in the opinion of Parliament this would occur.
Mr. Rose: Since your Commission accepted her as a. . . .
Mr. Juneau: I was going to. . . .
Mr. Rose: I am sorry, I did not mean to interrupt there.
Mr. Juneau: . . . continue answering your question. So starting from that, what we interpreted to be the spirit of the act, when we looked at the CRTC and the Legal Branch of the CRTC as well as the kind of work that has to be done, we found, for instance, that almost every month, if not every week, the lawyers of the CRTC have to make at least preliminary decisions concerning controversies involving political parties, and individual radio stations. I have here a list from August to December of about 12 or 15 cases where the Legal Branch has had to make decisions concerning controversies between political parties and radio or television stations.

Mr. Blair: Mr. Chairman, I simply wanted to say this with reference to Mr. Rose's question. Since I represent an Ottawa constituency I have been very concerned about the application of the Public Service Act and I have a written ruling from the Public Service Commission which says that a member of the public service cannot belong to a political party which I rate in the same way as the determination expressed sometime in the last few months that a public servant cannot have a sign on his lawn in support of a political party.

Mr. Juneau: In my simple judgement . . . I interpreted the act to mean that there are cases where usefulness is impaired by the fact that the objectivity of the person is put in doubt by the parties who are administered by the CRTC or any other commission. I was going to give you—at your request—a certain number of examples of that kind of interpretation made by the legal counsels of the CRTC. I can give them to you or not give them to you.
Mr. Rose: Let us have them, Mr. Chairman.
The Chairman: I think perhaps there would be a willingness, Mr. Juneau, to have you give us one or two examples of this in addition to the one you have already given.
Mr. Juneau: I gave you one. I said an opinion to another station interpreting the provisions of the act relating to a broadcaster who is a candidate for election. On September 30, 1971:

> Participation of Assistant Counsel in meetings with political parties concerning distribution of time on the CBC network during a provincial election.

This takes place all the time. Our lawyers have to meet with the political parties and the broadcasting stations on the sharing of time. They have to make decisions then which can be appealed. They are not really decisions—they are not final—but they have to give very important advice in very controversial situations involving political parties and broadcasting stations.

Mr. Nowlan: As you are aware, there are employees of the Commission who were defeated candidates for the various parties.
Mr. Juneau: I am not aware of that.
Mr. Nowlan: Well, I certainly am aware of it.
Mr. Juneau: Employees of the Commission?
Mr. Nowlan: Employees of the Commission. You are not aware of other employees who were defeated candidates for the Liberal Party and perhaps for any other party, but I am speaking specifically of the Liberal Party.
Mr. Juneau: No.
Mr. Nowlan: I am surprised at that because I ran against one who is now an employee of the Commission and is a very fine individual. This is why I am completely at cross-currents here because I can sympathize with the dilemma you are in.

Mr. Lussier: (Commissioner of the Public Service Commission)

It is with an open mind and a trusting attitude that we approach each case. The statistics speak for themselves. Since the Act came into force, we have given favourable decisions in over 90 per cent of the cases.

However well intentioned we may be, we must respect the wording and the intent of the Act which you, members of Parliament, have entrusted to us for implementation. What does the act specifically state?

> . . . the Commission may, if it is of the opinion that the usefulness to the Public Service of the employee in the position he then occupies would not be impaired by reason of his having been a candidate for election . . . grant to the employee a leave of absence without pay to seek nomination as a candidate and to be a candidate for election. . . .

The wording is clear. What about the intent? It seems equally clear to us. It does not behoove us, as those entrusted with implementation, to decide that this legislation has no real effect. We have to find its true significance by reference, if necessary, to the debates which led to its enactment. The legislation requires us to identify situations in which a public servant might no longer, as a result of specific political activities, be as useful to the Public Service as he was before. Since the legislators in their wisdom have concluded that there do exist positions of a nonpolitical nature, and since they have entrusted us, the Public Service Commission, with the responsibility of identifying these positions, we ourselves have to establish certain basic criteria. Ranking first among these criteria is the fact that a public servant has or does not have functional contacts with political groups, or parties. We take it for granted that Parliament did not intend that public servants, in the discharge of the discretionary duties assigned to them, should expose themselves to criticism in the area of political partisanship. . . .

The present description of [her] duties had already made us aware of the discretionary nature of some of Miss Eaton's functions. But it was proper for us, before reaching a decision, that we should consult with the deputy head concerned, who is actually in the best position to know the true nature of the applicant's duties. You are already acquainted with the opinion submitted to us by Mr. Pierre Juneau, Chairman of the Canadian Radio Television Commission. The opinion reinforced the decision which we felt to be the proper one after reading the statement of duties.

We had to accept the obvious and recognize that, in the event of Miss Eaton's not obtaining the nomination or being defeated in the election and returning to a job, she would have found herself in the very situation which the legislation had in mind and wanted to avoid. In compliance with the letter and the spirit of the law, we have reluctantly denied leave of absence without pay.

Mr. De Bané: I would now like to ask whether the Public Service Commission, at the time of Miss Eaton's appointment, was aware of the fact that she had previously engaged in political activity and, whether this information would, under the terms of the law, have in any way influenced your decision?

Mr. Lussier: As I see it there are two aspects to your question. First, did we know? When we examine the files of lawyer candidates, it is natural for us to examine their application forms. If the applicant has not mentioned any type of political activity, we do not speak of it. It is none of our business. We take it for granted that every citizen is free. When a person comes to us, he has only to say: I have such and such a quality.

If the applicant mentions in his curriculum vitae, by way of a personal note, that he has taken part in political activity of some sort, we ask him whether it be party organization or running for office, if he is to become a lawyer in our department.

I will give you some figures covering the past four years. We have interviewed and offered jobs to some 200 candidates. And when we asked some of them, that is those who declared that they had been involved in political activity in the past, whether they were willing to cease their political activity, none of them refused.

Now for the second part of your question: "if you had known would you have appointed her anyway?" We have to bear in mind the act which we have just read. The act states the Commission shall take this into account when dealing with a candidate who is already a public servant. The law does not require that we take this fact into account when the candidate is not at the time of his application a public servant. We are not holier than the pope.

As a rule we do not take this into account, generally speaking. I do not know whether I have answered your question or not.

Mr. Lussier: Section 32(3) states:

> (3) Notwithstanding any other Act, upon application made to the Commission by an employee the Commission may, if it is of the opinion. . .
>
> . . . this is our opinion. . .
>
> . . . that the usefulness to the Public Service of the employee in the position he then occupies would not be impaired by reason

> of his having been a candidate for election as a member described in paragraph (1)(a), grant to the employee leave of absence without pay to seek nomination. . . .

We have to grant this leave to allow him or her to seek the nomination as a candidate.

. . . and to be a candidate for election . . . and so on. I would like to tell you, sir, that we wanted to be—I do not like to use the word 'liberal'—but as broad as we could in the interpretation of the act. We asked the Justice Department whether it would be possible for us to grant two kinds of leave: one to allow a person to seek the nomination and another one to allow the person to seek candidacy. That means that she will not be deprived of her duties or of her employment for a longer period. . . .

Here is the end of the opinion of the Department of Justice:

> I am of opinion that subsection (3) of Section 32 of the Public Service Employment Act envisages the granting of a single period of leave in respect of the nomination and election campaign of an employee and that it would not be in accordance with that subsection to grant two shorter periods of leave. I am further of opinion that a person seeks nomination at the time he places his name before a nominating convention or otherwise seeks to secure his nomination as a candidate.

Unfortunately, we were defeated.

Mr. McCleave: She (Miss Eaton) is without a position at the present time, I understand.

Mr. Lussier: Unfortunately, she is suspended.

Mr. McCleave: She is suspended. Does that mean that she can go back to her work if she ceases these activities to become a candidate?

Mr. Lussier: This would depend on her Deputy Minister at the moment. She has not been fired yet.

Mr. McCleave: I see. All right. Well, this was the refinement that I was trying to make between Section 32 (1) and 32 (3).

Mr. Lussier: That is not a reflection of opinion, sir; it is only because she may be fired only by the Treasury Board.

Mr. McCleave: Perhaps she has some friends there; I hope so anyway.

The Chairman: Nobody has friends at Treasury Board.

The Chairman: Would it then be fair to say that there are no practical guidelines in effect for public servants as to who may or may not be a candidate, that there are no practical guidelines in effect as to who has a sensitive position and who has not, when it comes to being a candidate for a political party? In other words, when people accept a promotion or accept a job they do not know that they may be writing themselves out of an active political career?

Mr. Charron (Assistant Director General, Staffing Branch, Public Service Commission): I think we would have to say that, being a

guideline, it is not a hard and fast rule. But that is, in fact, a guideline. We can say, based on our experience with the legislation since 1967, that positions in the executive category, some positions in the administrative and foreign service category, and some positions in the professional and scientific categories are sensitive.
The Chairman: Are they defined anywhere?
Mr. Charron: Listed as such, no.
Mr. Lussier: No, we have only guidelines and we cannot have more than that.
The Chairman: That means that any employee in the federal public service does not know until he makes an application whether or not his candidature is going to be approved by the Public Service Commission?
Mr. Lussier: I would not say so so flatly, because they have more than an intuition.
The Chairman: Could you elaborate on that?
Mr. Lussier: If somebody is offered a promotion we do not usually tell him, "Do not forget that if you accept that promotion you will not be allowed to enter politics." No, we do not do that. But we may say quite naturally that these people who are granted these sensitive positions, who are graduating to sensitive positions, know that by instinct.

Appendix I
Public Service Employment Act
Political Partisanship.

32. (1) No deputy head and, except as authorized under this section, no employee, shall

(*a*) engage in work for, on behalf of or against a candidate for election as a member of the House of Commons, a member of the legislature of a province or a member of the Council of the Yukon Territory or the Northwest Territories, or engage in work for, on behalf of or against a political party; or

(*b*) be a candidate for election as a member described in paragraph (*a*).

(2) A person does not contravene subsection (1) by reason only of his attending a political meeting or contributing money for the funds of a candidate for election as a member described in paragraph (a) of subsection (1) or money for the funds of a political party.

(3) Notwithstanding any other Act, upon application made to the Commission by an employee the Commission may, if it is of the opinion that the usefulness to the Public Service of the employee in the position he then occupies would not be impaired by reason of his having been a candidate for election as a member described in paragraph (*a*) of subsection (1), grant to the employee leave of absence without pay to seek nomination as a candidate and to be a candidate for election as such a

member, for a period ending on the day on which the results of the election are officially declared or on such earlier day as may be requested by the employee if he has ceased to be a candidate.

(4) Forthwith upon granting any leave of absence under subsection (3), the Commission shall cause notice of its action to be published in the *Canada Gazette*.

(5) An employee who is declared elected as a member described in paragraph (*a*) of subsection (1) thereupon ceases to be an employee.

20
The Renfrew Group

In 1973, a Commission was established under Part II of the federal Inquiries Act "to investigate and report upon the state and management of that part of the business of the Department of Manpower and Immigration" relating to a number of immigration matters in Montreal.

One of the matters investigated by the Commission was the activities of what the Commission called "the Renfrew group". This group was composed of fourteen persons who entered Canada from India on non-immigrant visas to work for Dey Yarns of Renfrew, Ontario.

Dey Yarns was incorporated under a federal charter on March 23, 1972 for the purpose of manufacturing metallic yarn. At this time, K. L. Dey, the company's founder and president, was twenty-seven years old. He had come to Canada from Goa as a landed immigrant in 1967.

In February, 1972, Dey was assisted in his application for a loan from the Ontario Development Corporation by B. J. Grant, Executive Director of the County of Renfrew Economic Development Branch. Grant also helped Dey to get a $50,000 loan from the Renfrew Industrial Commission on April 28, 1972. Moreover, three members of the Industrial Commission, including Grant, personally backed a bank loan of $25,000 for Dey. This loan was repaid when the Ontario Development Corporation on September 11, 1973 disbursed to Dey a loan in the amount of $175,000.

The Department of Regional Economic Expansion signed an agreement on November 1, 1972 approving a loan to Dey of $98,765. This amount was based on $1,000 for each of the estimated fifty jobs which would be created plus 15 per cent of the approved capital of the eligible assets of $325,000. Dey never received this loan from the Department because his plant never began commercial production.

In 1971, Dey had purchased machinery for the manufacture of metallic yarn (zari machines) from a company in India owned by the Kaid family who were friends of Dey. Then in March, 1972, Dey bought a building in Renfrew for $60,000 and declared that production operations were under way.

In the meantime, Dey made frequent visits to India and in January, 1971, during one of these trips, the Kaid family helped him to recruit employees for his proposed company. He supported the applications of a number of potential employees before Canadian immigration officials in New Delhi and fourteen applicants who eventually received non-immigrant one-year visas all arrived in Canada between March 16, 1972 and February 22, 1974.

However, the interviewing officers at the Canadian immigration offices in New Delhi had recommended against approval of the applications. In early November, 1971, the officers telexed the Immigration Foreign Service in Ottawa that the applicants were not skilled workers, they spoke little or no English, they had not signed contracts for employment in Canada, they were not aware that their work in Canada was supposed to be training Canadians to use zari machines, and their real purpose in coming to Canada was to become permanent residents. The telex stated specifically: "We would like assurance that these people are not being victimized and be sure that cheap labour is not being imported which would be rather embarrassing to the Department with the present rate of unemployment." In view of this assessment, Mr. W. A. Roberts, Acting Director of Operations, Immigration Foreign Service, issued instructions on November 10 that no action be taken on the applications before further investigation was undertaken.

Then on January 12, 1972, Mr. Grant wrote to Mr. V. N. Woods of the Ontario Region Manpower Division of the Department questioning the assessment given by the officers in New Delhi and requesting that the applicants be granted work permits. In later testimony before the Commission, Grant said that Dey had shown him the telex from New Delhi and that his questioning of the contents of the telex was based on information received from Dey.

On January 24, Roberts sent a telex to the New Delhi officers saying that the "matter has been investigated and we are satisfied that these men are urgently needed. . . ." He also stated: "Can understand your reticence but in view of employment possibilities in an area already suffering from underemployment it is being recommended that . . . . these people be allowed to proceed as non-immigrants. . . ." Roberts testified before the Commission that his recommendation was based on the assurances he received from the Ontario Region Manpower Division. These assurances were evidently based on Grant's January 12 letter to Woods. When Roberts was asked by the counsel for the Commission what the division of authority was between himself as Acting Director of Operations and the Manpower branch, he replied: "Just liaison. Manpower carried out investigation in the field and my responsibility was solely to transmit instructions to our offices overseas." Counsel for the Commission observed during his questioning of Roberts that

> . . . What Manpower appears to have said is that . . . you had an area in which there was unemployment and the proposed plan had indicated . . . jobs would be created. The people in New Delhi, however, were assessing another matter, and that is the competence of twelve people who appeared before them to do what it was contended they would do and their bona fides. It would appear . . . that they were considering two different things and that the Manpower evaluation had nothing to do with the evaluation in New Delhi.

Eight members of the Renfrew group testified before the Commission that they learned in January 1971 that Dey and Ram Kaid were seeking workers for Canada and that for 25,000 rupees (about $3,300) these workers could get permanent residence in Canada. They were promised a non-immigrant visa permitting employment at Dey's factory for an assured salary of $400. per month, air fare to Canada, and food and lodging upon their arrival in Canada. Each of the eight paid part of this money on account in India and part after arrival in Canada. By the time the Commission began hearing evidence in November, 1974, these eight persons were all landed immigrants and were fully employed and well-established in Canada. The other members of the group denied that they had paid any money. These persons were not landed immigrants at the time of their testimony to the Commission. They merely held extensions of their non-immigrant visas, could not apply for landed immigrant status and were still employed by Dey. The Commissioner concluded that "these witnesses were not frank with the Commission. I believe that they, like the others, paid money before leaving India, but did not wish to reveal that fact because they were still employed by Dey and were subject to his power and authority, and because they wanted desperately to remain in Canada but were under constant threat of deportation."

All members of the Renfrew group did testify that their real aim in coming to Canada was to stay permanently and that Dey had promised them that they would be granted permanent residence.

Dey testified before the Commission that he had paid the workers the promised amount of $400. per month and their Income Tax T-4 slips showed that amount. The workers claimed that they had received only $200. per month. It appears that at the beginning Day gave each worker a monthly cheque of $400. He then insisted that these cheques be endorsed over to him and he gave the workers $200. in cash. After September 1974, the date when Dey was called to testify before the Commission, he paid his workers the full amount of $400. When the workers were asked by the Commission why they did not make more of a fuss about this situation, one testified that "every people know all the things that he was cheating us and doing everything. But he told us that if we want to go back to India like that, so, we don't want to go, we want to stay here."

Ten of the fourteen members of the Renfrew Group worked for varying lengths of time at Dey Yarns. When the Commission began hearing evidence in November, 1974, however, the company employed only three of the workers brought from India plus one secretary and one "salesman". The Commission concluded, despite Dey's claims, that production never got under way. In February, 1975, Dey Yarns Limited went into receivership and a trustee was appointed. The plant was closed and was subsequently rented as a warehouse. The machinery was sold for scrap for $2,595.12. Counsel for Dey informed the Commission that Dey had left Canada for an indefinite period.

A journalist who commented on all these events in one of Canada's major newspapers asked these questions: "What went wrong here? Who is responsible? What can be done to prevent similar incidents in the future?"

21
The Minister and the Doctor

In October 1971, Information Canada published the third volume of a three-volume report entitled *The Bankslanders: Economy and Ecology of a Frontier Trapping Community*. Volume 3, subtitled *The Community*, analyzed the current status and future prospects of the community of Sachs Harbour which is located on Banks Island in the Northwest Territories. Chapter three of this volume described a well-publicized controversy in 1970 between the federal government and the native people of Sachs Harbour in regard to the potential impact on the community of oil exploration on Banks Island.

The inside front page of the report contained a statement that "the opinions expressed in this report are those of the author and not necessarily those of the Department of Indian Affairs and Northern Development" as well as the words "Issued under the Authority of the Honourable Jean Chrétien, P.C., M.P. Minister of Indian Affairs and Northern Development." The report was written by Dr. Peter Usher, a social scientist employed by the Department.

In the Preface to volume 3, Dr. Usher stated that

> the social scientist is expected to employ accepted scientific methods in collecting and analyzing his data. . . . This does not mean, however, that his analysis is "objective" or value free. Indeed it cannot be, nor ought it to be so. The ultimate application of social science is the solution of social problems, and these can be neither identified nor solved without reference to personal and societal values. . . . Since I have been associated with the community of Sachs Harbour over a period of six years, I have not written a value-neutral report. I can only express the belief that my biases have not caused me to obscure or ignore pertinent data or conclusions.

The first three chapters of volume 3 were entitled respectively "Sachs Harbour: 1965-1967," "The Encroachment of Government," and "Oil and Trapping." These chapters contained criticism of government and departmental policy toward the community of Sachs Harbour. In the fourth and final chapter, entitled "Conclusions and Recommendations," Dr. Usher observed in relation to the fur economy that

> the near total reliance in government planning on the new economic sectors, and the consequent neglect of the fur industry, has rendered the latter option virtually untenable for most northerners at present" and he recommended that the government "examine the

possibilities of re-establishing the fur industry in the North, and develop plans for maximizing the industry's contribution to the northern economy.

In regard to community autonomy and control, Dr. Usher noted that

> While the extension of many government and private services to the North has been beneficial, the overwhelming control and direction of these by outside personnel and institutions can lead to a serious breakdown of local autonomy and initiative at both the individual and community level. . . . At Sachs Harbour, and probably elsewhere as well, the government has much to overcome in re-establishing a healthy working relationship with native northerners.

With respect to non-renewable resource development, Dr. Usher stated that "the potential for conflict between present land-based activities, and oil or mineral exploration and development must be fully recognized." He noted further that

> 1. The legitimate interest of native people in their land and resources must be fully recognized.
> 2. All possible harmful effects of oil and mineral development on the environment, and particularly on wildlife resources, must be fully investigated *in advance of* actual development work. . . . The cost of these investigations may perhaps legitimately be charged to oil and mineral companies. The research itself, however, must be conducted by disinterested parties, and made public so that it can be evaluated by any individual or group. Government cannot prejudge the outcome of such research and must be prepared to adjust development plans on the basis of the research results. . . .
> 3. Government (and industry) concepts of "consultation" must be completely revised. The Banks Island controversy, and other similar ones, suggest that for government," consultation now means merely informing people of pre-existing plans and suggesting ways in which they should adapt to them. This is often accompanied by attempts to inform and educate which . . . appear as propaganda campaigns. Such "consultation" is becoming increasingly unacceptable to native northerners. It should be replaced by *negotiation,* in which interest groups may bargain as equals and have equal access to information as well as to technical and negotiating expertise.

Dr. Usher recommended a moratorium on oil and mineral development in all areas utilized by native peoples until the conditions outlined above were met. He concluded that "since it is primarily government which has failed to meet these conditions, government must bear full responsibility for the resulting delays and inconveniences to other parties." Native people should not be obliged "to pay for previous government negligence with their own livelihoods and communities."

On February 1, 1972 about five months after the publication of volume 3 of the report, the *Toronto Star* quoted Jean Chrétien, the Minister of Indian Affairs and Northern Development, as follows:

> For a white man from the South (Usher) to say they (the Eskimos) made the wrong decision is a bit paternalistic. He seems like the typical white man who knows what is best for the Eskimos.

On February 2, the CBC program "World at Six" reported that

> Peter Usher, one of the few social scientists to earn the respect of the native people in the Western Arctic, was criticized by his boss Northern Affairs Minister Jean Chrétien. Mr. Chrétien called a paper on the island situation "a shabby piece of research."

Then on March 5, the following exchange took place on the CTV program "Question Period":

> Jean Chrétien: No, it's two completely different problems completely because in the parks we say that we'll permit the natives who use those areas already for hunting and fishing ground to keep on using them as they have done over the last few years, or many, many years. The question of Dr. Usher's report was really to the Banks Island problem and I think that . . . the facts that he elaborated in his document didn't match the conclusion because he said that the oil explorations were not hurting at all the wildlife on the island so . . . .
> Question: Was that a Government Report?
> J.C.: Yes . . .
> Q: And yet it's nonsense (you're in effect saying)?
> J.C.: Yes, but I never claim that all the people that work for us are very bright. Sometimes they make mistakes.
> Q: Dr. Usher is stupid, is he?
> J.C.: His conclusions were, yes.

On March 10, Leslie Barnes, Executive Director of the Professional Institute of the Public Service of Canada, sent a letter to Mr. Chrétien demanding that he retract his statements about Dr. Usher and apologize publicly to him. Sections of the letter read as follows:

> The Professional Institute is concerned that you, a Minister of the Crown, should apparently see fit to attack publicly in such offensive and opprobrious terms, a public servant who has no means of defending himself. If you have been reported correctly, your action is even more reprehensible when deliberately aimed at a young public servant who is a member of your own Department and who wrote the document under your direction and under the supervision and control of your senior officers. Indeed, your actions were not only ill-considered but carefully calculated, since you apparently attacked

> the document and its author on different occasions and over a period of several weeks.
>
> Dr. Usher's considered conclusions are based on hard evidence covered in the report, and while it is your prerogative not to agree with the policy implications of his conclusions (as is made clear in the standard disclaimer at the front of the report), it is surely inappropriate for you to attack his conclusions without bringing to bear the weight of opposing scientific evidence and interpretation. . . .
>
> A Minister of the Crown assumes responsibility for the activities of his Department and the work of his employees. . . .
>
> The Institute also considers your public attacks on Dr. Usher as a threat to the scientific and professional integrity of its members. It would be a most unhealthy situation if professional public servants were afraid to perform their duties fully and honestly, through fear of having their professional reputations and careers blasted in public, particularly by those in authority over them.

In the House of Commons on March 15, Mr. Erik Nielsen, a Progressive Conservative member from the Yukon, asked Mr. Chrétien if he intended to "apologize publicly to Dr. Usher and concede that the remarks were inappropriate." Mr. Chrétien said that the report "was published at the request of Dr. Usher who was attacking the government. Obviously he could expect me to reply, because I do not usually let myself be attacked without defending myself." Mr. Neilsen then asked if Mr. Chrétien would "concede that his description of Dr. Usher's conclusions as being stupid was wrong and that it was indeed not a shabby piece of research as the minister alleged." Mr. Chrétien replied that he had read the report and when he was asked what he thought of it, he had answered with his "well-known frankness."

On March 16, *The Globe and Mail* reported that outside the House on March 15 Mr. Chrétien said that if Dr. Usher "had not wanted to be criticized in return, . . . he should have come to him confidentially, instead of going public." Mr. Chrétien said also that Dr. Usher had complained that the Eskimos' flourishing trapping industry was being endangered but in fact trapping had been better on the Arctic island since the oil companies arrived.

22

A "Miner" Problem

Shortly after a provincial Obudsman took office in 1967, he received a complaint from Mike Jenson, a former coal miner. Jenson's complaint concerned a house which he had owned and which had been constructed on Crown property under lease to a private coal company. He claimed that when the lease had terminated, the house was sold without his knowledge and before he had an opportunity to move it off the property. He stated also that for several years he had tried unsuccessfully to obtain financial compensation from the Department of Lands and Forests. Jenson's solicitors, who believed that all other avenues of appeal had been exhausted, recommended that he take his grievance to the Ombudsman. The Ombudsman's inquiries revealed the following information.

The Department of Lands and Forests issued a Townsite Lease to a coal company for a period of twenty-one years beginning February 1, 1953. Jenson, who worked for the company as a miner, built a house on the Lease (the leased Crown property). The house was recorded in the company's files in Jenson's name as Building #158.

In 1957, an inspector for the Department of Municipal Affairs sent a letter to his deputy minister in regard to the ownership of private houses for 1957. The letter was accompanied by a corrected list of assessments for homes on the Lease and the list included Jenson's name and house. Records for 1957 also show that Jenson paid both school and property taxes on the house during that year. The tax notice from the Department of Municipal Affairs referred to Jenson as the "owner" of the house. In 1958, Jenson rented his house when he left the employ of the company and also left the area.

In late 1961, the provincial government agreed to the company's request that the company surrender its Lease with the Crown. The conditions of the cancellation of the Lease included a requirement that a public notice, approved by the Director of Lands of the Department of Lands and Forests, be placed in a local newspaper and in a newspaper in the provincial capital, to notify property owners of the action being taken. By this time, Jenson was no longer a resident of the area and claimed that he did not see the notice. He also claimed that when he rented the house, he left notices on the door, on the wall and on the ceiling providing his forwarding address. (No evidence was available to confirm or dispute these claims.)

Mr. Jenson stated that during a visit to the area, he had been told by the caretaker of the property that the houses on it were to be moved. He decided therefore to move his house to a nearby town and to sell it. He said that he had employed a house mover to move his house for him. He said also that he intended to clear the brush from his house to the nearest road to facilitate the moving of the house. An investigator from the Ombudsman's office tried to locate the house mover and finally learned that he had died in 1963.

In the meantime, the company made a contract with a construction company for demolition and clean up of the Lease. This work was to be "under the direction, control and supervision of the local District Forester" (an employee of the provincial Department of Lands and Forests). The company contracted to place in trust with the Crown a cheque in the amount of $16,000. The cheque was to be released to the independent contractor upon completion of the demolition and clean up "to the local District Forester's satisfaction."

Jenson said that he had returned to the area two or three weeks after he had arranged to have his house moved in order to begin clearing the brush. However, he found that his house had disappeared. He learned that the house had been sold and moved to a community not far away. By the time the Ombudsman received Jenson's grievance the house had changed hands at least once and was being used as a residence by the present owner.

The Department of Lands and Forests turned down Jenson's claim for compensation for the loss of his home. The Department stated that Mr. Jenson had no right or claim to the house he had built and therefore he had no claim against the Crown. The Department wrote to Jenson's solicitors as follows:

> Your client must be presumed to have been fully aware of the following facts if and when he undertook to build the house he now claims:
>
> a) the land on which it was situated was not owned by him;
> b) he had no permission or authority of any kind to build it on the lease; and
> c) he had no right, express or implied, to remove it at any time.

Before deciding what action to take on the basis of all this information, the Ombudsman referred to the relevant sections of the Ombudsman Act which set out his responsibilities. The Act included the following provisions:

> 11. (1) It is the function and duty of the Ombudsman to investigate any decision or recommendation made, including any recommendation made to a Minister, or any Act done or omitted, relating to a matter of administration and affecting any

person or body of persons in his or its personal capacity, in or by any department or agency, or by any officer, employee or member thereof in the exercise of any power or function conferred on him by any enactment. . . .

20. (1) This section applies where, after making an investigation under this Act, the Ombudsman is of the opinion that the decision, recommendation, act or omission that was the subject matter of the investigation
   a) appears to have been contrary to law, or
   b) was unreasonable, unjust, oppressive, improperly discriminatory or was in accordance with a rule of law or a provision of any Act or a practice that is or may be unreasonable, unjust, oppressive, or improperly discriminatory,
   or
   c) was based wholly or partly on a mistake of law or fact,
   or
   d) was wrong. . . .

20. (3) If, where this section applies, the Ombudsman is of opinion
   a) that the matter should be referred to the appropriate authority for further consideration, or
   b) that the omission should be rectified, or
   c) that the decision should be cancelled or varied, or
   d) that any practice on which the decision, recommendation, act or omission was based should be altered, or
   e) that any law on which the decision, recommendation, act or omission was based should be reconsidered, or
   f) that reasons should have been given for the decision, or
   g) that any other steps should be taken, the Ombudsman shall report his opinion and his reasons therefor to the appropriate Minister and to the department or agency concerned, and may make such recommendations as he thinks fit and in that case he may request the department or agency to notify him within a specified time of the steps, if any, that it proposes to take to give effect to his recommendations.

23
The Resigning Engineer

Mr. Wilfred Gretton, the Director of Personnel for a large government department, learned that a young engineer named Ron Elgun had submitted his resignation.

Although Mr. Gretton knew that Elgun was not considered to be one of their most effective engineers, he did believe that Elgun had some real promise. Gretton did, therefore, want to do everything he could within reason to keep the engineer from leaving government service. He immediately asked Elgun to come in to see him and began the interview by explaining that it was his custom to see all employees who resigned so that he could learn as much as possible about "personnel relations" in the department.

Elgun stated in a matter-of-fact way that he had already given a great deal of thought to the matter of resigning before he submitted his formal resignation. As Gretton inquired about Elgun's work, it soon became apparent to Gretton that Elgun's desire to quit was based mainly on one incident. Elgun explained that he had prepared a report for his boss, the Chief Engineer, and had included in the report certain information that revealed some errors in judgement by the Engineering Section. The Chief Engineer had "suggested" to him that he might delete this embarrasing information and "smooth over" that portion of the report. Elgun had felt very strongly that compliance with the Chief's request would be against both his professional principles and his personal ethics. Elgun told Gretton that he had not been able to sleep because of the worries and conflicts involved in making a decision on this matter.

Elgun went on to explain that he had discussed the issue with professional colleagues in other organizations, both in the government and in the private sector. The characteristic type of advice he had received was "Don't stick your neck out" and "It's not your funeral." But Elgun said that "it is my funeral. If anybody who really knows this field were to read my report, he would think that I don't know my job."

Gretton asked if the facts to be deleted are really so important. Elgun declared most emphatically that while nothing can probably be done about it now, the facts were of grave importance at the time and must therefore be included.

Elgun said that he had gone to Toronto on the previous weekend to discuss the matter with his parents. He had tried to make them understand that he didn't want to be dishonest, but neither did he want to be disloyal. And he certainly did not want to be regarded as an engineer who didn't know his job. "About all my father would say," explained this very troubled young man, "was that jobs like mine are hard to get and that I should think of my responsibility and obey my superior. My mother got all worked up about it. She said that if I lose my job, it will be a disgrace to the whole family. She reminded me that none of my relatives of the past three generations has ever lost a job. She wept, of course. She couldn't think of anything but the possible disgrace to the family. Dad seems to think I'm crazy. He says there's no room in business today for what he calls foolish ideas."

"What makes you so sure," Gretton asked, "that you are going to lose your job just because you are honest?" Elgun remained quiet for a moment, and then he said: "The Chief Engineer thinks he has all the answers. And he seems to do just about anything he wants to. You just can't buck a guy like this. I know!"

"You know this is to be a fact?" inquired Gretton. Elgun then said that he had heard about a man who had lost his job a couple of months after openly disagreeing with the Chief Engineer. Gretton asked for the man's name and called the personnel records unit for the relevant file. Then, after consulting the file, he explained that the man had, in fact, resigned in order to increase his salary by joining a private company. "Well, that may be," Elgun mumbled, "but if your records showed the true facts, the Chief probably made it so hot for the guy that he quit just to get out of the mess."

Elgun paused. Then he said: "Ok, you're right of course, I don't *know* it for a fact; but I do know my boss. He is inflexible. He is always right. Nobody can tell him anything. *Arrogant* is his middle name. I don't have any doubt that he'd find it damn easy to make it really hot for me if I ever tried to buck him." Elgun paused again. Then he continued rather thoughtfully. "You know John Dewey, the philosopher, says that there is one main distinction between a bad man and a good man: the bad man is the one who begins to deteriorate, no matter how good he has been; the good man is the one who, no matter how bad he may have been, moves to become better." Following a large sigh, Elgun said: "I've made up my mind. The only thing an honourable man can do is to sever all connections. There are some dirty messes that aren't worth trying to clean up."

24

The Foot and Mouth Disease Epidemic, 1952*

On November 26, 1951, Mr. Charles Blair, a farmer near McLean, Saskatchewan, telephoned the veterinarian at Indian Head about his ailing cattle. He told the veterinarian that three of his thirty-four cows were not eating, that their milk production was dropping off and that they had blisters on their tongues. The veterinarian was ill and couldn't come out to see the cattle so he prescribed a laxative by telephone. Blair got the medicine and had two neighbours come in to help him administer it. By this time he noted with alarm that twenty-four of his cows were sick, and on November 30 he called in another veterinarian, named Dr. T. Craig, from Regina.

Dr. Craig drove the thirty miles from Regina the same day and on his return to the city he contacted the Regina office of the Health of Animals Division of the federal Department of Agriculture. On December 2, two federal officials, Dr. A. Landry and Dr. S. Campbell, drove with Dr. Craig to the Blair farm. Dr. Landry was the Assistant Veterinary Director of the Regina office and Dr. Campbell was one of the inspectors. Dr. R. Thompson, the Veterinary Director in Regina, gave his professional staff almost complete freedom in their work. Dr. Campbell took charge of the diagnosis of the sick cattle. He gathered material from the mouths of the ailing cows and brushed it on the tongues of two horses. Horses are even more susceptible than cows to vesicular stomatitis, a fairly common cattle disease which was suspected in this case. On the other hand, horses are immune to foot-and-mouth disease, a dread cattle plague. On this same day, Ottawa was informed by Dr. Campbell that a suspected contagious disease had been discovered and the Blair farm was quarantined. (See Appendixes I and II.)

By December 8, Dr. Campbell thought he had found that the two inoculated horses had developed small blisters on the tongues and gums while the cows had apparently recovered from their illness; this confirmed his earlier diagnosis of vesicular stomatitis. So on this day the quarantine was lifted.

On December 12, the two neighbours who had helped Blair with his cattle found they had sick cows and these two farms were quarantined. The diagnosis was still vesicular stomatitis, and when the sick cattle had apparently recovered two weeks later, the quarantine was lifted. In the meantime the Rhodes packing plant in Regina reported sick cattle and on December 18 the affected animals were isolated and quarantined, but

*The names of all government employees have been changed.

when they appeared to recover they were passed for slaughter. It was noted that Blair had sold five calves to Rhodes on November 23.

On January 15, Dr. P. Bailey, Veterinary Director General and head of the Health of Animals Division of the federal Department of Agriculture, came to Regina to address the annual meeting of the Saskatchewan Livestock Board. He visited the Rhodes plant on January 17, the day the quarantine there was lifted. Dr. Bailey discussed the disease outbreak with local men and evidently dismissed alarmist views. He was reported by a local vet as saying: "You boys are looking for bears behind every bush." When interviewed in Ottawa some time later, Dr. Bailey could not remember using the expression. On the other hand, he pointed out to a Committee of the House of Commons:

> We have always cautioned our men not to use the term 'foot-and-mouth disease' loosely. We know the implications . . . . We know right well how it would affect international trade and affect the whole national economy. However, we did not suspect there would be foot-and-mouth disease up there. It was absolutely preposterous—2,000 miles from anywhere that you would expect it. You would expect it at some of our coasts at our quarantine stations, but not out there.

In the meantime the disease was spreading. A veteran journalist who visited the area and studied the outbreak wrote:

> But now (after January 15) the disease began to spread in earnest. It cropped up in a dozen new herds, most of them west of Regina along Wascana Creek into which the Rhodes plant sewage is emptied. Cattle were much sicker now—blisters were bigger, recoveries slower, the spread through individual herds much faster and more complete. Horses were still not catching it. Except for those 'several vesicles on tongues and gums' of two Blair horses on December 8 not a symptom had shown on any horse. People were worried by this. Farmers began asking if veterinarians were sure this wasn't foot-and-mouth disease to which horses are immune. Vets themselves began to have doubts. One Regina practitioner says that Dr. Landry, the government vet, wrote 'more than once' to Dr. Bailey urging that the diagnosis be checked in the Animal Pathology Laboratory, which is at Hull, Quebec.

In an interview with the journalist, Dr. Bailey did not recall that anyone had suggested to him that the disease might be foot-and-mouth disease or that the lab tests should be made.

The last foot-and-mouth outbreak in Canada had been in the late 1890s, while the last large outbreak in the United States had been in 1929. Cattlemen in the United States were more familiar with this disease than were Canadians for they had experienced four large epidemics since the First World War. One of these plagues alone had cost the states of California and Texas 163,800 animals. Those cattlemen who were familiar with the disease were very much afraid of it. The disease has a morbidity of one hundred per cent and its virus can survive for months under the right conditions. They knew that it can be imported from central Europe, Spain, South and Central America, Asia or Africa at any time for in these areas the disease has never been eradicated and it is always present. It can be spread by direct contact of animals or by transfer of saliva, blood, milk, raw meat, meat products and so on. The only sure test to discover the seven varieties of the disease is to inoculate blood specimens with serum. This serum is available to Canada from England by international agreement and it can be flown over within twenty-four hours.

Evidence before a parliamentary committee indicated that from January 4 to February 12 no written communications were exchanged between the Ottawa head office and the field office in Regina. (See Appendix III for the organization chart of the Department.) Nevertheless, in the first week of February, Dr. F. Knight, Director of the Production Branch of the Department of Agriculture and Dr. Bailey's immediate superior, informed Mr. B. Davies, Deputy Minister of Agriculture, of the outbreak of cattle disease in Saskatchewan. In his appearance before the House of Commons Committee, Mr. Davies stated that

> . . . the first information came to me verbally from Dr. Knight and it would be during the first week of February . . . . I took no special action at the time. Dr. Knight first reported to me that this vesicular stomatitis was in Regina; but at that time Dr. Knight informed me of what action was under way and it seemed to me to be sufficient—so I gave no further directions.

On February 11, Dr. Bailey went on statutory leave. On February 12, a telegram was received by his deputy, Dr. J. Broom from Dr. Landry in Regina indicating that the situation "appeared to be really serious, and requested assistance to verify or refute his suspicions." Dr. Broom called Dr. Bailey at his home and was told to get in touch with Dr. D. Saunders, Chief of the Department's Animal Pathology Division, and request him to send one of his pathologists to Regina to conduct tests and if necessary to bring material to the Hull lab for further testing. Dr. Saunders reported this call to the Committee of the House of Commons:

> My first knowledge of it was on February 12 when Dr. Broom phoned me and asked if I had heard about vesicular disease in Western Canada. Well, I had not heard about that disease. Then he went on to say that Dr. Landry took a rather dim view of the whole prob-

> lem and Dr. Broom suggested that I send someone out west to view these animals. I told him that in my opinion this would be a waste of time. Vesicular diseases are treacherous and the only sensible thing was to get specimens as soon as possible and because we have a virus unit all the necessary work can be done perfectly safely. Therefore, the logical step was to send those specimens in. Dr. Broom agreed with that and four days later specimens arrived. In the interval, however, in fact on the 13th of February, I radiogrammed to England and asked them to send out here our serum which was sitting there in the refrigerator.

When questioned by members of the committee, Dr. Saunders stated categorically that he had not had any previous communication about this outbreak with any official of the department.

On February 15, Dr. Bailey came into his office to pick up his mail and he noted that Dr. Broom had asked the Regina office to send specimens in to the Animal Diseases lab in Hull. From his home that night he sent a wire countermanding this order, because as he told the Committee of the House: "It is very, very dangerous exposing foot-and-mouth disease virus to hazards of transportation. . . ." On this point Dr. Saunders testified:

> Q. In your opinion, Dr. Saunders, is it dangerous procedure having these samples sent from the field to the laboratory at Hull?
> A. No, I would not recommend it if I thought it was dangerous.
> Q. It was also stated by one of the witnesses yesterday that it had been Department of Agriculture policy as long as he remembered, that these samples be not sent to the laboratory at Hull. Did you know of any such ruling?
> A. No. I know of no such ruling; it has been common practice to send samples with consent or under instruction from the head of the branch or head of the division. I know that we have received vesicular samples over the years.

In any event, the countermanding wire by Dr. Bailey was too late. The specimens had already been forwarded. From these specimens Dr. Saunders was in a position to report to Dr. Knight by February 18 that the disease must be treated as foot-and-mouth disease until further tests had confirmed or negated the preliminary results. By February 24, the virus had been identified beyond all doubt as foot-and-mouth virus, type A.

In the meantime, Dr. Bailey had returned to work and with one of his senior officials had flown to Regina. The cattle on the Blair farm were inoculated with foot-and-mouth virus and only 7 of the 38 head showed any signs of infection. This was conclusive proof that 31 head had been exposed to the virus earlier.

A major operation was then begun to stamp out the disease which by now had spread to 21 municipalities. A very vigorous campaign was conducted involving stern measures and as a result the epidemic was halted and the disease exterminated. (See Appendixes I and II.) Six months later, on August 19, the area was declared free of the disease. In the meantime, the following steps had been taken:

1. The 21 municipalities involved were quarantined and another 41 municipalities were put under a modified quarantine. This quarantine lasted from February till August.
2. The livestock from 42 premises which were suffering from the disease were slaughtered. This involved the killing of 1,343 cattle, 293 swine, 97 sheep, 1 goat and 7,372 poultry. The compensation value of these animals was $503,000. The slaughter involved the digging of pits eleven feet deep with bulldozers, the animals were driven into the pits and killed with rifles by members of the R.C.M.P. and the carcasses were then covered with lime and buried.
3. The 42 premises had to be disinfected. All loose litter, straw, hay, feedstuffs, feedboxes, wooden floors, troughts, etc., had to be collected and burned. Barns and other outbuildings and their surroundings were drenched with a strong lye solution. Manure piles had to be burned or buried. The yards had the tops shaved off by bulldozers, the top soil was buried and the yards then drenched with lye solution. Farm equipment and machinery and such animals as horses, cats and dogs were washed with a sodium carbonate solution.
4. Precautions were tightened in March to prevent the import of this virus. A skeleton staff of Agriculture officials at seaports was radically increased until eventually more than 70 officials were supervising the arrival of immigrants at ports and airports and the import of cattle, other animals, meat and meat by-products, hides, skins, etc., and the disposal of refuse from ships and airplanes. Their scrutiny was particularly directed toward conveyances arriving from countries where foot-and-mouth disease had not been conquered.

The total costs of the eradication campaign, including compensation, was estimated at $977,600, but the really big costs came in other forms. The United States imposed an embargo on the import of all Canadian livestock which was not lifted until March 1953. The cost of this embargo to Canada was estimated at over seven hundred million dollars.

An investigation was made by the Department of Agriculture and by the Royal Canadian Mounted Police to ascertain how this virus had come to Saskatchewan. It was ascertained that an immigrant from an infected area in Western Germany had come to Regina on November 2 and he had been sent to the Blair farm by immigration authorities to work as a farm hand. It has been surmised that this immigrant, Gunther

Schmidt, may have carried meat foods such as German sausages with him to the farm. Schmidt had not been satisfied with the employment offered by Mr. Blair and had left on November 5. In his subsequent wanderings he had been in southern Manitoba, in northern Ontario and other parts of Canada and he was picked up in Vancouver in March 1953. He was brought to Ottawa where his clothing and effects were thoroughly examined at the Hull lab but all results were negative. The surmise is, however, that he was the source of the virus and it appears most fortunate that no other area in Canada was infected by him.

The whole issue of the epidemic became a matter of considerable public interest and political debate. As a result, the House of Commons Standing Committee on Agriculture and Colonization held an inquiry to determine what went wrong and who was responsible for what occurred. (See Appendix IV for extracts from the evidence submitted to this Committee.)

Appendixes

I. Excerpts from the Animal Contagious Diseases Act
II. Excerpts from the Animal Contagious Diseases Regulations
IV. Organization Chart of the Department in 1952
IV. Extracts from evidence presented to the Standing Committee of the Canadian House of Commons on Agriculture and Colonization.

Appendix I

Excerpts from the Animal Contagious Diseases Act, Chap. 9.

16. There may be appointed in the manner authorized by law such inspectors and other officers as are necessary to carry out the provisions of this Act.

17. Such inspectors or other officers, on receiving information of the supposed existence of any infectious or contagious disease among animals, shall proceed to the place mentioned with all practicable speed, and execute and discharge their duties pursuant to the regulations made under the authority of this Act and the instructions received by them.

18. Any such inspector or other officer may, at any time, for the purpose of carrying into effect any of the provisions of this Act, enter any place or premises, or any steamship, vessel or boat, or any carriage, car, truck, horse-box or other vehicle used for the carriage of animals, but shall, if required, state in writing the grounds on which he has so entered.

19. (1) Where an animal infected with or labouring under any infectious or contagious disease, or suspected of being so affected is sold, disposed of, or put off, or is exposed or offered for sale in any place, or is brought or attempted to be brought for the purpose of being exposed or offered for sale in any market, fair or other open or public place where other animals are commonly exposed for sale, any clerk or inspector, or other officer of the fair or market, or any constable or policeman, or any other person authorized by the mayor or reeve, or by any provisions of this Act with respect to infected place shall apply to and have effect in respect of such lands and buildings as if the same were actually within the limits of the infected place.

25. (1) The area of an infected place may, in all cases of a declaration by the Minister, include any common, field, stable, cowshed or other premises in which infectious or contagious disease has been found to exist, and such area as to the Minister seems requisite.

(2) The Minister may, from time to time, by order, extend or curtail the limits of an infected place beyond the boundaries of the common, field, stable, cowshed; farm or premises where infectious or contagious disease is declared or found to exist.

26. The area of an infected place may, in any case, be described by reference to a map or plan deposited at some specified place, or by reference to townships, parishes, farms, or otherwise.

27. The Minister may, at any time, upon the report of an inspector, by order, declare any place to be free from infectious or contagious disease; and thereupon, and from the time specified in that behalf in the order, the place shall cease to be deemed an infected place.

28. An order of the Minister relative to an infected place shall supersede any order of a local authority inconsistent with it.

29. The provisions of this Act with respect to infected places shall not restrict the moving of any person, animal or thing by railway or other mode of transport on highways through an infected place, if such person, animal or thing is not detained within the infected place, unless such transport is prohibited.

30. Whenever under this Act a place has been constituted an infected place, no live animal, nor the flesh, head, hide, skin, hair, wool or offal of any animal or any part thereof, nor the carcass nor any remains of any animal, or any dung of animals, nor any hay, straw, litter or other thing commonly used for and about animals, shall be removed out of the infected place, without a licence signed by an inspector, until said place has been released by order of the Minister.

Appendix II

Excerpts from the Animal Contagious Diseases Regulations, Part VII.

99. (1) Whenever the Minister is of opinion that a serious outbreak of an infectious or contagious disease has occurred in any area in Canada, he may issue a declaration to that effect in which he shall designate the area, the disease and the animals likely to be affected thereby, and from the issue of the declaration until the Minister issues a further declaration declaring that the infectious or contagious disease is under effective control, no person shall, without the permission of an inspector or such other person as the Minister may designate in the declaration, move

(*a*) any such animal
  (i) into the designated area
  (ii) out of the designated area, or
  (iii) from one place in the designated area to another place in the designated area, unless both places are owned or occupied by the same person,

(*b*) any flesh, hides, hoofs, horns or other parts of such animals, or in the case of poultry the eggs thereof, or any hay, straw, fodder or other things used for feeding or caring for such animals or any cereal grain
  (i) out of the designated area, or
  (ii) from one place in the designated area to another place in the designated area, unless both places are owned or occupied by the same person.

(2) Any permission given by an inspector or such other person designated by the Minister may be general or particular.

(3) Subsection (1) does not apply in respect of the movement out of the designated area of anything in an elevator, as defined in the Canadian Wheat Board Act, on the date the Minister's declaration comes into force.

100. The Minister may require that any designated animals, carcasses or portions thereof, eggs, or any articles used to hold or convey such animals, carcasses, portions or eggs, or anything contaminated or suspected of being contaminated with the disease designated pursuant to section 99, shall be treated, dealt with or disposed of in such manner as the Minister may direct.

101. Her Majesty in right of Canada or in any other right is bound by the provisions of the Part.

Appendix III

ORGANIZATION CHART OF THE DEPARTMENT IN 1952

DEPARTMENT OF AGRICULTURE

MINISTER OF AGRICULTURE
Rt. Hon. J. G. Gardiner

DEPUTY MINISTER
B. Davies

INFORMATION SERVICE
- Press, Radio, Films, Exhibits
- Departmental Publications
- Departmental Library

AGRICULTURAL PRICES SUPPORT BOARD

PRODUCTION SERVICE—D. Knight
- Administration
- Health of Animals Division—P. Bailey
- Livestock and Poultry Production Division
- Plant Products Division
- Plant Protection Division
- District Offices throughout Canada

DEPARTMENTAL ADMINISTRATION
- Financial Control
- Foreign Agricultural Relations
- Office Services
- Organization & Personnel
- Procurement
- Property, Buildings & Equipment
- Race Track Betting

REHABILITATION SERVICE
- Maritime Marshland Rehabilitation Administration-Amherst
- Prairie Farm Assistance Administration-Regina
- Prairie Farm Rehabilitation Administration-Regina

SCIENCE SERVICE—G. Lyon
- Administration
- Animal Pathology Division—(one lab in Hull), D. Saunders
- Bacteriology Division
- Botany and Plant Pathology Division
- Chemistry Division
- Entomology Division
- Forest Biology Division
- Branch and Regional Laboratories and Offices throughout Canada

EXPERIMENTAL FARMS SERVICE
- Administration
- Animal Husbandry Division
- Agriculture Division
- Cereal Crops Division
- Field Husbandry, Soils and Agricultural Engineering Div.
- Forage Crops Division
- Horticulture Division
- Illustration Stations Div. Husbandry Division
- Tobacco Division
- Branch Farms, Stations and Special Laboratories throughout Canada

MARKETING SERVICE
- Administration
- Consumer Section
- Markets Information Section
- Transportation & Storage Section
- Dairy Products Division
- Economics Division
- Fruit & Vegetables Division
- Livestock Products Division
- Poultry Products Division
- District Offices throughout Canada

Appendix IV

The material that follows is extracted from the evidence presented to the Standing Committee of the Canadian House of Commons on Agriculture and Colonization, *Proceedings,* Ottawa, Queen's Printer, 1952. The evidence has been edited and rearranged:

Mr. B. Davies, Deputy Minister of Agriculture, testifies:
Mr. Chairman, it has been suggested that a brief statement on the organization of the Department of Agriculture, with particular reference to the place of those divisions concerned with the control of disease, would be helpful to the committee. First, the department consists of operating units which might be described as commodity divisions. These divisions in turn are grouped under administrative heads on something approaching a functional basis. The main groups are, Production, Marketing, Experimental Farms and Science Service. In addition, there are the other administrative groups having to do with rehabilitation, marshland and prairie, and the price-of-support function of the Prices Support Board and the Prairie Farm Assistance Act, but I am not mentioning them further because they have no part to play in this particular examination. The Production Service is the one within which the Health of Animals Division functions. The other major divisions in that production service are Livestock and Poultry and Plant Products. These divisions, all of them, deal with production matters or matters that affect production. In the main, they have to do with the promotion, control and protection of animals and crops, and not with the marketing, and not with scientific research. They are, therefore, mainly enforcement and administrative divisions. The Health of Animals Division of the Production Service, then, is a division of the department which administers the Animal Contagious Diseases Act, the Meat and Canned Foods Act, and all of the regulations made under those Acts. They are essentially a protective and enforcement organization. Now, the other main division to which you may wish to direct your attention is the Animal Pathology Division, whose main job is research into animal diseases and all the things related thereto. In addition, that division does routine testing and checking and supplies laboratory services generally to the Health of Animals Division and some other divisions that require that type of service. I should have told you, Mr. Chairman, that the Health of Animals Division is headed by Dr. P. Bailey, who is described as Veterinary Director General, while the Animal Pathology Division functioning within the Science Service is headed by Dr. D. Saunders, who is chief of that division, with laboratories not only in Hull, where the headquarters are, but at various other points across the country.

Perhaps only one other point need be made in order to make this whole position clear, and that is that the heads of the two divisions to which I have referred, namely Dr. Bailey and Dr. Saunders, report respectively to Mr. Knight, who is director of the Production Service, and to Dr. Lyon, who is director of the Science Service; and those officers in turn report to the deputy. The grouping of divisions to which I have referred was made in 1937-38, and the purpose of that grouping at that time was to bring together research and scientific organizations in one broad group, and administrative and enforcement divisions in another broad group.

Mr. Diefenbaker: I would like to ask Mr. Davies one or two questions. He has told us that Dr. Bailey and Dr. Saunders report to Mr. Knight and to Dr. Lyon and that they in turn report to him as deputy minister. What was the date of the first report received by you, through these gentlemen, Mr. Davies, in regard to the outbreak of some disease among animals in the Regina area?

A. I do not think I can give you the exact date, Mr. Chairman, because the first information came to me verbally from Dr. Knight and it would be during the first week of February.

Q. And up until the first week of February then, Mr. Davies, you had received no report . . . ?

A. No report that made sufficient impression on me in any event to stay in my mind.

Mr. Wright: As a result of any reports you received was there any action you took with regard to this yourself, as deputy minister?

The Witness: No, I took no special action at the time Dr. Knight first reported to me that this vesicular stomatitis was in Regina; but at that time Dr. Knight informed me of what action was under way and it seemed to me sufficient—so I gave no further directions.

Mr. Argue: Did you, Mr. Davies, discuss with any of your officials in February as to what should be done with samples from infected animals—whether those samples should be subjected to tests within the area where the disease was prevalent or whether they should be sent to the Hull laboratory?

A. I do not recall any further discussion at that time.

Q. You were never aware of any discussion or any arguments or any differences of opinion as to whether certain tests should be made in Saskatchewan or whether certain other tests should be made at the Hull laboratory?

A. I do not recall any further discussion at that time.

Mr. Diefenbaker: Well, Mr. Davies, tests were made in the field and, according to the records produced yesterday, on February 14th there was a telegram from Dr. Landry, assistant district veterinarian, advising that vesicular specimens were being forwarded by air express. Then, on February 15th there was a wire from Dr. Bailey to Dr. Thompson (district

veterinarian) countermanding the gathering of specimens and the delivery of such specimens to Hull for analysis or examination. Was a matter as important as the countermanding of instructions that had already been given by Dr. Landry to Dr. Thompson—was that matter brought to your attention in order to get your authority or to discuss it with you?
A. No, I had no knowledge. It was an order dealing with a technical point and in the normal routine that would not come to me.
Q. A lot of this work was being done in the field by the officers of your department . . . is it not customary that reports are made regarding these investigations by these people to their departments through the senior officers of the department to the administrative head?
A. Yes, that is the practice . . . . The routine is that the district veterinarian reports to the veterinarian director general weekly, I believe.
Q. Now the reason I am asking you that is this. Would you not have expected Dr. Thompson to have reported to Dr. Bailey in this weekly report what he was finding, what was taking place—the extension of the disease and so on?
A. Yes.
Q. Now, from January 4, 1952, until February 12, there is no report whatsoever. Doesn't that strike you as being strange?
A. There should be reports—the weekly reports from Dr. Thompson.
Q. And if there are no such reports do you regard that as concrete evidence that somebody was not discharging his responsibility?
A. I would like you to ask Dr. Bailey that question about weekly reports. I have no personal knowledge of that because I do not see them.
Q. But then wouldn't you expect as deputy minister in a matter as serious as this that some time between January 4 and February 12 indications would be made to you in writing, setting forth the seriousness and the potentialities of this disease, and the possibility of this disease being more than stomatitis?
A. No, I wouldn't, in view of the fact that Dr. Broom and Dr. Knight were both in the same building and could see me daily, and most of the discussions on a matter of that sort would be verbal.
Q. I have just one other question. Have you known of other cases where the orders made by one incumbent of the senior position have been countermanded by the official head on his return following vacation?
A. I do not recall any at the moment, Mr. Chairman.
Mr. Cote: In sequence to questions put by my honourable friend, I would like to ask the witness one question, as to whether it is the government's responsibility, or whether it is a civil servant's responsibility, and I want to put the guy on the spot who is responsible. Now, if he thinks that there is another than himself, I would like to know; I would like to know the goat.

The Chairman: Mr. Davies considers he cannot answer your question, Mr. Cote.
Mr. Cote: Now, I do not think the Minister is responsible. I do not think the government is responsible. I think civil servants are responsible. I would like to know who, and I would like to see him fired.
The Chairman: That, Mr. Cote, is the business of the committee.
Mr. Diefenbaker: And when did you first report to the Minister of Agriculture about the situation in regard to the disease, whether it was suspected to be stomatitis or foot-and-mouth disease?
A. I think it was on the 18th of February when I first reported to him.
Q. And at the time you reported to Mr. Gardiner, was it true that he was away on vacation?
A. He was in the west, on the west coast, I think.

(Selected from evidence of Dr. P. Bailey, Veterinary Director-General of the Canadian Department of Agriculture)

Mr. Chairman and hon. gentlemen: First I feel that I should give you a brief outline of the duties and responsibilities of the Health of Animals Division so that you may be a little clearer in your mind as to what procedures are followed in dealing with various things.

We are responsible for keeping track of the disease situation in all countries of the world. We get reports from various countries with which we have trade relations about the disease situation. We at least get monthly reports and if there is anything serious which occurs we get them more often.

We then have certain safeguards to prevent the introduction of those diseases into Canada. That is, livestock come in under a permit, which is issued under the authority of the Minister. And if a country is not declared to be free of the serious animal diseases, that country does not get a permit. In any case, if the animals do come in on a permit, they are placed under quarantine and they go to a quarantine station for a certain period of time.

From various countries we receive shipments of hides and such like, countries which have foot-and-mouth disease and rinderpest; but they come into Canada in a certain way; if they are hard dried, there is no danger of disease. But if not, there are restrictions, and they go to a tannery where they are disinfected; they come in under seal, the seal of the car is broken by an officer of the department, and the hides are processed and disinfected under supervision.

In addition to that, of course, there are some 115 or more packing plants in Canada which are under departmental supervision and inspection. And to give you an idea of what goes on at those plants, I mean what the supervision is of animals which are sent in there for slaughter for food purposes, they receive an ante-mortem inspection.

In addition to that, of course, plant supervision means this: that all steps from the time the animal is driven into the plant and slaughtered until the finished product is packaged are under supervision.

Dr. D. Saunders, Chief of the Division of Animal Pathology:
Turning to our actual contact with this episode; my first knowledge of it was on February 12 when Dr. Broom phoned me and asked if I had heard about vesicular disease in Western Canada. Well, I had not heard about that disease. Then he went on to say that Dr. Landry took a rather dim view of the whole problem and Dr. Broom suggested that I send someone out west to view these animals. I told him that in my opinion this would be a waste of time. Vesicular diseases are treacherous and the only sensible thing was to get specimens as soon as possible and because we had a virus unit all the necessary work can be done perfectly safely. Therefore, the logical step was to send those specimens in. Dr. Broom agreed with that and four days later specimens arrived.

In the interval, however, in fact on the 13th of February, I radiogrammed England and asked them to send out here our serum which was sitting there in the refrigerator. It arrived about three days later, so that actually the serum arrived before we were ready for it.

All this leads up to the inoculation of horses, pigs, cattle, guinea pigs and chick embryos, all to determine whether it was foot-and-mouth disease virus and as soon as we had any tissue to harvest, serological work commenced. By the time the 18th arrived we were beginning to take a dim view of the episode as we thought our animals were coming down in a manner which very much suggested foot-and-mouth disease virus. So I phoned Mr. Knight's office (Director of Production Services—under which the Veterinarian General's division was placed) or perhaps he called me that morning and I told him the results, also that I thought they should consider it tentatively as foot-and-mouth disease until we had an opportunity of studying it in some greater detail.

We ran a second series of animals to make absolutely sure. We ran five serological tests in all, and we came up with the same answer, namely, that here we had in our presence foot-and-mouth disease virus, type A. That was, of course, reported immediately . . . on the 24th. I think there is nothing to add to that and I turn now to a problem that has been forced on my doorstep, namely this wretched Blair's diseased herd . . . . I suggested a method of dealing with this question, namely, the inoculation of type A foot-and-mouth disease virus into the tongues of these cattle . . . . I may say that proof and past experience with foot-and-mouth disease virus is that animals do not become infected when challenged with foot-and-mouth disease virus if they have recently been infected with this type of virus. Of these animals I found that there are 38 of them . . . . Thirty-one gave no reaction whatsoever to the inoculation of the virus—consequently those animals must have been infected.

Dr. P. Bailey, Veterinary Director-General, under examination:

Dr. Diefenbaker: Now, Dr. Bailey, I have looked over this file, that is the one in answer to the motion passed by parliament; and am I not correct when I suggest to you this, that between the 4th day of January and the 15th day of February you made no written communications with any official in the field or anywhere else within your department with regard to foot-and-mouth disease or stomatitis?

A. I don't think I ever communicated.

Q. No; and you, of course, were greatly concerned right from the beginning of this outbreak were you not?

A. I was quite concerned at first when I heard it was a vesicular disease, but knowing that there were men on the job who had seen both vesicular disease and foot-and-mouth disease, I was not very apprehensive.

Q. And, as you told us a moment ago, it is difficult to diagnose this foot-and-mouth disease?

A. Yes, it is difficult.

Q. You were fully on guard against the possibility of foot-and-mouth disease coming to Canada, were you not?

A. We want to be, sir.

Q. And you were throughout the years?

A. Yes.

Q. And being alert, did you throughout—and I am not going to ask you for particulars—but did you get good co-operation from all the officials in your department?

A. Yes, as far as I know, sir.

Q. And also from officials in any other sector or sections of the department?

A. Oh yes, yes.

Q. You asked for a report on the Rhodes' plant, did you not?

A. Yes.

Q. And, Dr. Bailey, you asked Dr. Thompson to provide you with Campbell's report?

A. Yes.

Q. And you received no wire from Dr. Campbell for several days, did you?

A. No.

Q. And then you got a report from Dr. Campbell which you produced yesterday?

A. I don't believe I have that with me. It is in our file and the date would be on it, stamped on it . . . .

Q. Well, if you will get that information and give it to us: (A wire was read) "AWAITING DR. CAMPBELL'S REPORT VESICULAR STOMATITIS RHODES' FEED LOT REGINA REPORTED WIRE OF DECEMBER 28 STOP LONG DELAY NOT UNDERSTOOD STOP PLEASE EXPEDITE REPEAT PLEASE EXPEDITE." You sent that wire?

A. Yes.

Q. You were very disturbed at the time because you had asked Dr. Campbell to make an early report?

A. Yes, it struck me that as the report did not appear in due time, to ask for a report.

Q. And you do not know when you got the report?

A. No, I could not say right now.

Q. You have already told the committee that you did not know when you got the reports on the various tests that were made; but, as a general rule, you were aware of the fact that in order to determine finally whether it was foot-and-mouth disease you had to have the results of these reports, and you would have to make certain decisions, did you not?

A. Yes.

Q. And you realized that serum had to be got from England?

A. Yes.

Q. Why didn't you get that serum from England?—and when I say "you" I mean your department. I am not speaking of you personally.

A. The serum was procured just as soon as it was thought that there was need for it.

Q. And with the spread of the disease into 11 places in January, in the face of that, no member of your department in the field or in Ottawa suggested that there should be further inoculations in order to determine the incidence of the nature of the disease; is that what you say?

A. I do not recall there being any suggestion along that line.

Q. And as I look over the record, am I not telling you what is a fact, that during the period, during January, all of those cases were arising, 11 cases, and in February, from the 1st to the 13th, there is not one letter from any official in Ottawa to the officers in the field regarding the seriousness of the situation?

A. No, there probably is not.

Q. Well, just for the sake of information, with a continually expanding disease as it was, . . . how did you keep these officials on the job, how did you alert them? How did you make them realize the seriousness of what was taking place?

A. We required a quarantine on all the premises affected.

Q. I see; but there were no instructions given whatsoever to the officials either to secure serum or to inoculate during that period?

A. If it is not on the record, that would be so.

Q. Now as soon as you went on your vacation, Dr. Saunders was left in charge?

A. No, Dr. Broom.

Q. And he is your assistant?

A. That is right.

Q. Now, almost as soon as you left, you know now that Dr. Broom, in collaboration with Dr. Saunders, issued instructions for the collection and forwarding to the laboratory at Hull of materials from the animals suffering from this disease; that was done; and from the record on what date was it, when they gave those instructions, according to the records in your department?

A. I think that is the 13th.

Q. And when did you first hear about it?

A. I think it was the 15th.

Q. And you came back rather unexpectedly on the 15th, did you not?

A. As a matter of fact, I came back to pick up some mail.

Q. And then you found out that during your absence Dr. Broom, who had taken your place, was acting in your place?

A. Yes.

Q. And Dr. Saunders had issued instructions for the collection of samples; and did you have any conversation with either of them?

A. I did, with Dr. Broom.

Q. And did you criticize him for the stand taken?

A. Not seriously, no. Any more than to indicate to him that I was very dubious about moving anything that might be serious, as I mentioned before when giving you the general picture, for fear of having it spread by either losing it or breakage on the way down.

Q. And then you countermanded his instructions?

A. Yes, I sent a wire.

Q. Did you tell him beforehand that you had put a stop to the whole thing?

A. No, because I did this from home at night.

Q. Mr. Argue: What happened to your order countermanding Dr. Broom's telegram? Was the material sent to Hull in spite of that order?

A. The material had been collected and sent before my telegram reached Thompson.

Q. And was the disease diagnosed on the basis of that material that came to the Hull laboratories?

A. I would say it was verified.

Q. That was the first verification?

A. That was the first time that it was officially designated as foot-and-mouth disease, after the evidence was all in.

(After a prolonged questioning of Dr. Bailey concerning the nature of various tests, Mr. Gardiner interposes on behalf of his officials.)

Right Hon. Mr. Gardiner: Mr. Chairman, I would like to speak on a point of order. It has been said on two or three occasions that the men we did this work in the field are going to be here . . . and those are the only men who can answer the questions. Dr. Bailey administers the head office here in Ottawa. He has responsibility for everything that is happening, in so far as we are responsible, from Halifax or from Newfoundland right through to Vancouver Island.

Now he has got a lot of other things to do besides this particular job. This job was done by the staff in Regina. Those are the men who are going to be available to this committee.

Now, it is all right to ask questions, then to turn around and say that means so and so and so and so; and to say these men never did make any tests on horses . . . . You take a pamphlet which says they should have done so and so, and then you say they did not do it.

Mr. Ross: They did not do it.

Mr. Gardiner: It is all right to say that when they are not here, but how does Dr. Bailey know whether they did it?

Mr. Ross: He should know.

Mr. Wright: On a point of order, Mr. Chairman. Yesterday, when we were questioning the Deputy Minister, Mr. Gardiner rose and said that he was not the right man to ask questions of and that Dr. Bailey would be before the committee.

Mr. Gardiner: Ask him the proper questions.

Mr. Wright: And he said that we would have an opportunity to ask these particular technical questions of Dr. Bailey who was the authority and who was the head of the department.

Now, when we have Dr. Bailey before the committee, the Minister tells us that Dr. Bailey is not the proper person to ask questions of but that we have got to get Dr. Landry or Dr. Campbell from Regina.

I suppose that when Dr. Campbell and Dr. Landry come from Regina we will be told that we have to get somebody else. Dr. Bailey is head of the department, and I think the questions that were being asked were quite legitimate questions.

Mr. Gardiner: That is correct, except for one thing. When I referred to the matter yesterday I was referring not only to Dr. Bailey; I said that the whole group of men from the department who were sitting behind me were here to be called. Dr. Bailey was the first one. He was called to outline the methods by which his department administers these matters . . . . I do not think it is fair to them for this committee to take a man who is not the man who carried out the work and to question him and insist on getting answers, and then have these men coming along later on and to tell them: well, your boss said so and so; now why are you saying something different.

Mr. Ross: The question the Minister raises right now does not satisfy me because he is apparently referring to the fact that some other officials would be better able to give the evidence, and that we will find the reports of the field men from January 4 to February 12 on the record. I would think that if the Minister had an efficient organization Dr. Bailey would have these reports from the field men under his supervision; apparently he has not got them, but that is the very question the Minister raised yesterday. Now that he finds Dr. Bailey cannot answer these questions he says: wait until we get the field men here. I say there is something grossly negligent in his organization of the department in that respect right there.

Mr. Diefenbaker: As far as Dr. Bailey is concerned, I have tried to keep from pre-judging the matter. . . . I am trying to listen to the evidence; but Dr. Bailey put on the record this afternoon and read from a record prepared, whether by himself or someone else, a complete recital of all these cases and what had been done; and he accepted and adopted what had been done as having been done on his behalf; otherwise, he could not have read all that. And I have just one word more to say to the Minister. No one can have any objections to the Minister being here, so long as he is not interfering with Dr. Bailey giving his evidence. Yesterday and today on a number of occasions the Minister was seen to be whispering with Dr. Bailey when questions were being asked. In my view that is an important thing and is not in accordance with the rules of this committee.

Mr. Gardiner: You are not my schoolmaster. When I was going to school if I were caught whispering I got rapped over the knuckles, but not from you.

Mr. Diefenbaker: I do not think the Minister should be whispering to Dr. Bailey when he is giving evidence.

Mr. Gardiner: I will whisper to anybody any time I like, even to you.

Dr. S. Campbell (Veterinary Inspector, Health of Animals Division, stationed at Regina) questioned:

Mr. Argue: You operate under the Animal Contagious Diseases Act, is that right?

A. Yes

Q. Are you aware of the provision of that Act? And would you say that the power there is under that Act to enforce a quarantine, is based on section 24 . . . ?

A. Yes.

Q. Did you at any time, since you made your first visit to the Blair farm and made a report on this disease, send in any report directly to the Minister, did you report to the Minister of Agriculture directly?

A. I made my report to my immediate superior, Dr. Thompson.

Q. Are you aware of the provision of the Act, section 25, subsection 1, which says:

> Whenever an inspector makes such a declaration of the existence or suspected existence of infectious or contagious disease of animals, he shall, with all practicable speed, send a copy thereof to the Minister.

A. I am aware of that.
Q. Why did you not send a copy of your report to the Minister as provided in the Act.?
A. It has never been our custom to do that; we make reports to our superior officer and he reports to the next in line.
Mr. Argue: I suggest, Mr. Chairman, there has been a serious breach of the law as applied to contagious diseases . . . .
Mr. Stewart: In all fairness to the witness and departmental practice you are not going to condemn this witness because he did not send it direct to the Minister . . . ?
Mr. Argue: Ultimately the Minister, after weeks, nearly a month went by, before he finally got it . . . . When the premises were quarantined first and an infectious disease established, the Minister should have been sent in compliance with the Act a copy of that report; and then again, according to the Act—and once more I am only a layman—but the Act provides when the quarantine is lifted it shall be by order of the Minister; and when the specific area in which the quarantine is established it shall be on order of the Minister?
Mr. Decore: Not "shall" but "may".
Mr. Argue: I have heard lawyers argue one way and another before—we have heard many times in government legislation "may" is mandatory.
Mr. Laing: Surely the Minister means the chain of command.
Mr. Argue: According to subsection 2(e) "Minister" means the Minister of Agriculture. The question I want to ask is this: In any of the general practices of your department in establishing a quarantine or lifting a quarantine, is it not the practice to have it by ministerial order?
A. Ministerial order covers the whole thing. It covers the general quarantine but not the individual quarantine.
Q. In this case the Minister of Agriculture had no knowledge of the lifting of the quarantine?
A. He certainly did. When this form . . . goes in (it) is forwarded with my report to Ottawa . . . . The Minister exercises his authority through the Veterinary Director General and issues a release which is mailed to the owner.
Q. . . . . when you speak of Ottawa you are not speaking of having sent or having received communication from the Minister of Agriculture—you refer to sending a report to the Veterinary Director General of his office?
A. I send my report to my head office in Regina and my superior in turn sends that report with all attached documents to the Veterinary Director General. The Veterinary Director General under authority of the Minister issues an order to terminate the quarantine.

Mr. Harkness: You said a while ago, Dr. Campbell, that you first were alarmed that this outbreak might be foot-and-mouth disease when you saw a pig in company with Dr. Landry, with a separated hoof?
Some Hon. Members: Hear, hear.
Mr. Harkness: I think my meaning is clear.
The Witness: I do not think Dr. Landry would quite agree with that.
Mr. Bryce: You better clarify the statement.

* * *

Dr. D. Saunders, Chief, Division of Animal Pathology, Ottawa, is examined:
Mr. Charlton: Dr. Saunders, in your experience as head of the Animal Research Division in Hull, do you feel you have always had the full co-operation of the Health of Animals Branch in anything that has been done?
A. Oh, yes, I think we have.
Q. And any time that the Health of Animals division thought it necessary to ask for your assistance and aid, that has been done?
A. Yes.
Q. Were you ever at any time up to the 12th of February consulted by any official of the Department of Agriculture (about foot-and-mouth disease)?
A. No, sir.
Q. In your opinion, Dr. Saunders, is it dangerous procedure having these samples sent from the field to the laboratory at Hull?
A. No, I would not recommend it if I thought it was dangerous.
Q. It was also stated by one of the witnesses yesterday that it had been Deparment of Agriculture policy, as long as he remembered, that these samples be not sent to the laboratory at Hull. Did you know of any such ruling?
A. I know of no such ruling; it has been common practice to send samples with consent or under instruction from the head of the branch or head of the division. I know that we have received vesicular samples over the years.
Dr. J. Broom, Assistant Veterinary Director-General of Canada, examined:
Mr. Argue: As Deputy Veterinary General, do you work in the same office as the Veterinary Director General?
A. Yes.
Q. Could you tell me what the internal procedure followed has been after an inspector in the field makes an investigation of an infectious disease, establishes a quarantine and files a report?
A. That inspector makes his report. He turns it in to the district officer in charge of the province. The district officer makes a record and any comment he makes is then forwarded to Ottawa, to the Veterinary Director General.

Q. And when the Veterinary Director General receives the report what is done with it then?
A. Well, it is recorded in our record room. The report is properly filed and if it is of an extraordinary nature it is passed on down the line.
Q. Passed on to whom down the line?
A. Well, the next man in line to be notified was the director of production service, and then the deputy.
Q. Mr. Knight was then the deputy. Do you know whether any of these weekly reports were sent to the Minister of Agriculture?
A. I would not be prepared to answer that question at the moment, sir, because I happened to be (absent), from the 27th of November to the 14th of January. I was ill, and away from the office, and in the interval anything that went on during that period was not known to me.
Q. There were some reports of the kind I have mentioned?
A. Yes, there would be some.
Q. And as far as you know, they were not forwarded to Mr. Young or the Deputy Minister?
A. Not that I am aware of.
Q. This seems amazing to me. I had asked the question yesterday of the witness about section 25, when an inspector makes such a declaration . . . I thought that meant directly to the Minister, but according to the opinion of Mr. F. P. Varcoe, Deputy Attorney General, in a submission given to the committee by the chairman today, that does not mean directly to the Minister . . . . Now, all that means to me is that . . . that a copy shall nevertheless go to the Minister through the departmental channels . . .
Mr. Gardiner: It is now settled by judicial authority that the Deputy Minister is the Minister, and the final decision on matters of law is a judicial decision.
Mr. Argue: O.K. If you want to assume it, and I do not assume it, the Deputy Minister in his evidence said those reports did not reach him until February . . . .
Mr. Stewart: Are you arguing to the Committee that we should have the Minister read reports received from over 25,000 veterinarian surgeons throughout Canada, that he should really read a thousand reports a day?
Mr. Argue: . . . it is my opinion that if these reports, very important reports on contagious diseases, had gone to the Minister personally, this situation would, in all probability, have been cleaned up and taken care of long before this, but because the law was not followed and because these reports did not reach the Minister throughout all the time of this disease until February 18th or so, it has led to the mess that we are in.

Dr. Davies, Deputy Minister, under examination:
Mr. Argue: . . . in your opinion did the Veterinary Director General use every possible precaution throughout the history of this disease?

Mr. Stewart: I do not think that is a proper question. On a point of order, Mr. Chairman. I do not know that one executive of the government should be asked a question as to the efficiency of another one. I think it is very unfair to ask one witness in the department whether the other fellow did everything that should have been done. We will decide that in the committee.
Mr. Argue: We will decide that on the basis of the evidence, and I think one of the most important pieces of evidence is the opinion of the work of that official by the Deputy Minister.
Mr. Decore: We can then go a step further. Probably this witness can give us his opinion of the Minister. Of course, we know your opinion of the Minister.
Mr. Argue: I have a high opinion of the Minister in a great many ways, Mr. Chairman. Are you going to rule that was an improper question?
The Chairman: No, Mr. Davies will answer your question. . . .
The Witness: Mr. Chairman, all I can say is that I have every confidence in Dr. Bailey and his organization. It is an extremely difficult thing to stand in public and pass judgement on a particular man and I would beg that the committee do not compel me to do that in too great detail. But we had an organization headed by experienced veterinarians who had come up from the bottom; not Dr. Bailey alone, Dr. Broom and Dr. Porter and Dr. Logan and Dr. Dillon; all men with experience and knowledge. We had similarly experienced and able men in the field. Now, any person who has to work with a human organization knows that all men in the organization are not equally able, and we all know that there are spots in every organization that are weak, because of the man who happens to be in a particular spot. If we had perfect men, and particularly if we had a perfect Minister and perfect Deputy Minister, we would have a perfect organization down below. We had, we thought, as good an organization as we could get.
Mr. Argue: Do you still think so?
The Witness: We had competent men in the field in charge of this work. Now judgement might be passed afterwards, as a matter of hindsight; but I must confess I do not know what else I could have done in the circumstances but to continue the confidence in these men that I had at the time and still have. That is as near as I can come to answering this question.
Mr. Wright: Dr. Davies, has any consideration been given in the department to merging, or placing under one head, the Department of Pathology and the Contagious Diseases Branch, and in your opinion would that result in closer co-operation between those branches?
A. That has been considered, Mr. Chairman. It was, in fact, the case prior to 1937 and 1938, when the present structure was set up. But the decision was then made, and it has since seemed to be a sound decision,

to bring the research services under one administration, and the enforcement and regulatory services under another. That condition prevails throughout the Department of Agriculture and I might say throughout other departments of government as well. You must decide on one form or other of organization in a particular situation and in this case these services have been grouped according to function. They both belong to the Department of Agriculture and there is no reason at all why there should not be complete co-operation among the branches or division, as the case may be.

Q. Would it be your opinion that if they had been under one head there would have been any different result in regard to this foot-and-mouth disease, or are you satisfied that there was the fullest co-operation between these departments in respect to this outbreak?

A. I have no knowledge whatever of any lack of co-operation between these two groups, and I have been in a position to see it, if it were true.

Dr. Bailey, Veterinary Director-General, under examination:

Mr. Cardiff: This afternoon when Dr. Davies was giving evidence, he admitted perhaps he was a little bit negligent in respect of reporting to the Minister at a certain time. Would you, Dr. Bailey, admit that you have been negligent at all in regard to the diagnosis of this disease in Saskatchewan?

A. No, I would not admit of having been negligent.

Q. You hold a very important position with respect to the livestock of Canada, do you not?

A. Yes, sir, which I appreciate.

Q. Well, would you tell me this. Why would it take you two months to decide whether you should take a test of this disease . . .?

A. I believe I have answered that question in various forms several times before. We did not think we were dealing with anything serious.

Q. Well, if you were not absolutely sure, would it not prompt you to take a test and be absolutely sure that you were dealing with a very contagious disease?

A. I was satisfied we were dealing with simple vesicular stomatitis or we certainly would have gone further, and quicker, with the tests.

Q. I admit that; but I still won't admit that it should have taken you two months to make sure that you were right; and if you will admit to me that you were negligent, I will quit asking you questions.
